D1434044

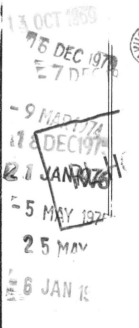

PEOPLE OF
GEORGIAN ENGLAND

PEOPLE OF
GEORGIAN
ENGLAND

Mary Cathcart Borer

ILLUSTRATED BY
William Randell

MACDONALD EDUCATIONAL

PUBLISHED BY MACDONALD AND CO. (PUBLISHERS) LTD.
49 POLAND STREET, LONDON W.1.

PRINTED IN GREAT BRITAIN BY
W. AND G. BAIRD LTD., BELFAST

CONTENTS

PLATES

George I

George II

George III

George IV

The Four Georges

Chapter One

THE BACKGROUND

When Queen Anne, the last of the direct line of Stuarts, died childless, in 1714, the throne of England passed to her German cousin George, a grandson of Charles I's elder sister, Elizabeth, who had married the German Prince Frederick of Hanover. George I was succeeded by his son George II, in 1727. George II's grandson came to the throne in 1760 and lived on into the nineteenth century, but during the last years of his life he was insane and his son George was appointed Prince Regent in 1811 and crowned George IV on his father's death in 1820. When he died ten years later his brother William, already elderly, succeeded, and on his death in 1837 King William's niece Victoria became Queen of England.

It is this period, from the accession of George I in 1714 till that of the young Princess Victoria in 1837, which we are calling 'Georgian England.'

George I was a German. He spoke no English and had little interest in English affairs. The Bill of Rights of 1689 had curtailed the power of the British monarchy and ensured that Parliament should have ultimate control of the government of the country, but for many years to come the King still had the right to appoint or dismiss ministers as he chose.

England was not yet a democracy for only a small minority of people yet had the right to vote. It was the landed and the rich who became members of Parliament and directed England's fortunes in foreign wars and foreign trade, and it was to be many years before they took responsibility for the

Liverpool in the early eighteenth century

well-being of the rapidly increasing numbers of the ordinary
people.

At the beginning of the eighteenth century the population
of England and Wales was only about five and a half million,
of whom more than half a million lived in the great commercial and cultural centre of London. The cities next in
importance to London, Bristol, Norwich and Liverpool, were
very small compared with the capital, with populations of
under five thousand, and most English people were still
country dwellers, living in their lonely hamlets, villages and
market towns, isolated by the difficulties of slow, horse-drawn
transport along ill-made roads which were often little more
than muddy tracks.

Though large tracts of the countryside had been enclosed
by the beginning of the eighteenth century, there were still
thousands of acres of unenclosed arable and common land,
where peasants and small farmers cultivated their strips and
grazed their livestock, as their forefathers had done since
medieval times.

By the end of the century more than three quarters of the population were still country dwellers and even as late as 1851 the proportion of town to country people was about fifty-fifty.

Though in many ways the eighteenth century was a violent age and people were still highly emotional and uncontrolled, it was an age of real if somewhat ostentatious elegance. It was a time of powder and patches, sedan chairs and handsome coaches, highwaymen and smugglers, of incomparable craftsmanship, of literature, painting and glorious music, of victories on foreign battlefields which gained a mighty empire and established a vast overseas commerce. It was also a time of scientific discovery and mechanical ingenuity and invention which, by the end of the century, had brought about the industrial revolution and set the course for England's industrial future.

The century left a great heritage of art and architecture but an even greater inheritance of social problems, as our manufacturing towns grew apace and the population with them. By 1750 it had risen to about six and a half millions, by 1800 to nine millions and by the time Queen Victoria came to the throne it was fourteen millions.

Few could have foreseen the transformation which the forces of mechanical invention were to bring. The problems they created came slowly at first, and it was not till a hundred years later, when they had assumed disastrous proportions, that serious attempts were made to solve them.

The new Hanoverian king, George I, was content to leave affairs of state to the Whigs, who were in power at the time of his accession, under the leadership of Sir Robert Walpole, and Walpole's outstanding ability raised him to the position of England's first prime minister.

James II had died in exile and Louis XIV had acknowledged his son, later to be known as the Old Pretender, as James III, the rightful king of England. Less than a year after George I's accession, there was a certain amount of

Tory support for the Old Pretender's persistent claim to the throne, but the Jacobite rebellion of 1715 petered out through lack of support. The new German king meant little or nothing to the people of England but they were on the crest of a wave of commercial prosperity and needed no change, least of all a return to the Stuarts. Through Marlborough's victories in the War of the Spanish Succession during Queen Anne's reign England had received Minorca and the strategic stronghold of Gibraltar, which gave us the vitally important control of the Mediterranean for our merchantmen trading with North Africa and the Levant. We also gained Newfoundland and the French colony of Acadia, which was renamed Nova Scotia, and were emerging as an important European power.

The War of the Austrian Succession

When George II succeeded to the throne he took as little part in affairs as his father and Walpole continued in office till his dismissal in 1739 for his unwillingness to take part in the next European struggle, the War of the Austrian Succession. George II, concerned for the safety of his Hanoverian possessions, himself formed an army of Hanoverian and English troops, financed with English money, to defeat the French and drive them from Germany: but two years later, in 1745, the English, Hanoverians and Dutch suffered a defeat by the French, who followed it by supporting yet another Jacobite rebellion in England. The Old Pretender was by now too old to fight but his son, the Young Pretender, landed in the Hebrides, in the forlorn hope of regaining the throne his grandfather had lost. The clans of the highlands rallied to him at first but the lowlanders remained aloof. As he marched south fewer and fewer Jacobites came forward to help him, and at the battle of Culloden Moor his army of five thousand highlanders was scattered by George II's redcoats. Bonny Prince Charlie fled back to the Hebrides and from there, with the help of Flora Macdonald, whose clan had

The end of the '45 rebellion – Bonny Prince Charlie and Flora Macdonald

suffered so bitterly at Glencoe half a century earlier, he eventually escaped to France, never more to return.

In prosperous, bustling London, with its newly built Mansion House, its theatres and coffee houses, its grand mansions in Mayfair and Belgravia, Covent Garden, Soho and Bloomsbury, there were few left to raise a toast to the forlorn cause of the Scottish prince, with a grievance that few but the elderly could remember.

India

In the early part of the eighteenth century the East India Company had only three small trading stations in India, where the cities of Madras, Bombay and Calcutta were later to be built. They were little more than groups of warehouses, each protected by a fort, manned by a few native soldiers in the pay of the company. When the War of the Austrian Succession broke out, the French governor of Mauritius besieged Madras, destroyed it, captured the clerks and merchants of the East India Company and imprisoned them at Pondicherry, the French station farther down the coast. Amongst these captives was a young clerk, Robert Clive.

India was a divided nation. During the sixteenth century the country had been almost completely under the single rule of the Mogul Empire, but by the eighteenth century the empire had collapsed, with independent, warring princes establishing themselves in separate states. The French planned a great French empire in India, with an eye particularly on the valuable rice, sugar and silk of Bengal, and they hoped to gain their objective by allying themselves with the rebel princes, but the English identified themselves with the cause of the Emperor.

Clive escaped from the French prison at Pondicherry and made his way to Madras, to become leader of the small army which the East India Company was hastily forming, and under his command they succeeded in capturing Arcot, the capital of the Carnatic, from the native prince who had been installed there by the French.

The Seven Years War

With the end of the War of the Austrian Succession and the treaty of Aix-la-Chapelle in 1748 there were a few years of peace in Europe but in 1756 war broke out again, this time Maria Theresa of Austria joining with France and Russia against Frederick of Prussia and George II of England.

News came from Bengal that the native governor, an ally of the French, had seized the East India Company's settlers in Calcutta and thrown a hundred and fifty of them into one small, airless, prison cell – the Black Hole of Calcutta. In the morning only twenty-three of them were still alive. Clive and his small army marched north from Madras to take revenge, and at the battle of Plassey they routed the governor's colourful infantry and cavalry. This victory marked the beginning of British ascendancy over the French in India, the ultimate withdrawal of the French and the founding of the British Indian Empire.

In North America and Europe, however, things were going badly. In North America there were about a million and a half people, with their quarter of a million negro slaves, settled in the thirteen English colonies by the middle of the eighteenth century. These colonies, each about the size of England, stretched in a long line down the Atlantic coast, east of the Alleghany mountains.

The French colony in Canada was firmly established along the shores of the St. Lawrence, centred on their cities of Quebec and Montreal, and France hoped for a North American empire stretching from the Great Lakes and the St. Lawrence southwards through the heart of North America to the basin of the Mississippi. In 1749 the governor of Canada had sent one of his officers, de Bienville, to claim the Ohio country between Lake Erie and New Orleans for Louis XV. De Bienville carried with him a number of tin plates and shields, inscribed with the arms of France, which were planted along the route or nailed to the forest trees, declaring that the land had been taken for France, but neither Indians nor

English took much notice. In that vast, lonely country they may not even have known what was happening. De Bienville returned to Canada and things went on much as usual.

The French then tried to win back Acadia, threatening the French peasants with excommunication and an eternity of perdition if they continued to owe allegiance to the English Crown, and at the same time they incited the Micmac Indians to harass the English settlers. The English replied by sending the French Acadians away from their farms, to fare as best they could amongst their compatriots in Canada.

When the French began a new drive from Lake Erie for the Ohio, the governor of Virginia sent a young officer, George Washington, with a small company of men, on a three months' journey through uncharted, snowbound forests and across frozen streams and rivers, to intercept them and warn them they must go no farther. The French disregarded the warning and the governor of Virginia appealed to England for help. After months of delay General Braddock of the Coldstream Guards arrived in Virginia and mustered a force which marched on the new fort which the French had built at the place where the town of Pittsburg was one day to arise. It was high summer by now and the long train of English wagons and tumbrils, ammunition carts and artillery, pack-horses and cattle made their slow way through the wild, uncharted mountain forests: and with them marched the Guards in their tight scarlet uniforms, pigtails and pipe clay, mitre hats and black gaiters, sweltering in the fierce heat of the American midsummer and burdened with their heavy, clumsy flintlocks: but they were ambushed by a force of French and Indians. Nearly two-thirds were killed or wounded and Braddock himself died of his wounds.

A few months later the formal outbreak of the Seven Years War intensified the conflict, but for the next two years matters went as disastrously for the English in North America as in Europe, where both Frederick of Prussia and the Duke of Cumberland were in retreat.

16

England's fortunes were at their lowest ebb when there came to the fore in the House of Commons a man who was to prove himself one of our ablest Prime Ministers, William Pitt. 'I know that I can save the country' he declared, 'and I know that no other man can.' He produced a plan for the campaign in North America which, under the brilliant leadership of Amherst, Lawrence and Wolfe, and culminating in Wolfe's famous capture of Quebec, systematically reduced the French to total capitulation, the French in Canada now finding themselves under British rule.

The year after the capture of Quebec, George II died. His eldest son had already died so his grandson, George III, succeeded, at the age of twenty-two, the first of the Hanoverians to be born in England and speak the language with ease. Young and arrogant, he dismissed Pitt and appointed Lord Bute in his place. When the war ended, in 1763, we had gained both Canada and India from the French and the following year British ships were exploring the Pacific and Captain Cook, in his travels from 1768 to 1771, was claiming all the new lands he touched – Australia, New Zealand and many of the islands of the Pacific – for the English crown.

The War of American Independence

To pay for the Seven Years War George III and his new Minister, Lord Bute, against the advice of Pitt and many others, insisted that the American colonies should pay various taxes, including customs duties on all goods sent out from England. The Americans refused. In 1766 Pitt was recalled to office, but he was a sick man and the following year he accepted a peerage and, as the Earl of Chatham, retired to the House of Lords.

The quarrel with America dragged on and the obstinacy of the colonists nearly settled the dispute, for by 1773 the only tax demanded of them was an import duty of 3d a pound on tea, payable when the cargo was landed: but when the next assignment of the East India Company's tea arrived at Boston the

The Boston Tea Party. The 'Sons of Liberty' tip £10,000 worth of tea into the harbour, rather than pay duty on it

Sons of Liberty, the organization founded to oppose British control, boarded the Dartmouth, burst open the crates of tea and tipped it all into Boston harbour. £10,000 worth of tea was destroyed and similar 'tea parties' took place at other ports along the eastern seaboard. English troops arrived in America. It was the signal for a war which, to the lasting chagrin of George III, we lost.

In 1776 the American States declared their independence. The war dragged on for seven more years but at last, in 1783, peace was made, America's independence acknowledged and Canada's boundary was moved back to its present line.

Many Americans who had remained loyal to England throughout the war were persecuted, whipped, tortured, tarred and feathered, dragged through horseponds, imprisoned and hanged. More than thirty-five thousand went over the border to Canada, where they were allotted land by the British government. About thirty thousand went to Nova Scotia and New Brunswick and others to the virgin country of Ontario, where they were soon joined by more United Empire Loyalists from south of the border. By 1791 there were twenty thousand English-speaking settlers in this new region, to the west of French-speaking Quebec province, and by act of the British Parliament Canada was divided. East of the Ottawa river was Quebec or Lower Canada, retaining its old system of French laws. To the west was the English-speaking Upper Canada.

France, still smarting under the defeat of the Seven Years War, gave open help to America during her war of independence, so that yet again England declared war on France. William Pitt, Earl of Chatham, was dead, but his son, William Pitt the Younger, took office and when he was only twenty-four became Prime Minister.

With the end of the American war, he set about making peace with France. He also put an end to the smuggling of wine, tobacco, tea and bullion which had become so widespread round our coasts, by the simple expedient of reducing the import duties to so small a figure that the smugglers efforts were no longer worth while and they were put out of business.

The French Revolution

The people of France, inspired by the successful fight of the Americans for freedom and long oppressed by the heavy taxes levied by Louis XV and Louis XVI, to pay for their long and disastrous wars, were on the point of rebellion. When the French Revolution broke out, in 1789, the people of France were determined to destroy not only the monarchy but the whole of the nobility from whom they had suffered for so long.

At first the revolutionaries had many sympathisers in Europe but as the struggle increased in violence and cruelty, feelings changed to horror and alarm. Fearing that the revolutionary spirit would spread beyond the frontiers of France, Prussia and Austria formed a coalition, demanding the restoration of Louis XVI. The order was defied and when Prussia and Austria invaded France the ragged armies of the Revolution not only repulsed them but overran Savoy and the Austrian Netherlands, while in Paris, during the September massacres, hundreds more aristocrats were guillotined.

Pitt tried to keep England out of the struggle but the English party agitating for war grew stronger, for those who had most to lose were panic-stricken. War was declared in 1793. On land we fared badly and by 1795 the Dutch Republic was affiliated to France. At sea, despite a mutiny in the navy against the appalling conditions below decks, we captured Ceylon and the Cape of Good Hope from the Dutch and repulsed an attempted invasion of Ireland by joint Spanish, Dutch and French forces. But when Austria signed a separate peace, we were left to wage the war alone, a small if pugnacious nation, with a population which was considerably less than a quarter that of the French.

The Napoleonic Wars

The young Napoleon Bonaparte was fast rising to power in France and the war developed into a struggle against a great military conqueror whose armies were spreading with terrifying relentlessness throughout Europe and the Mediterranean to Egypt. Nelson's outstanding victory of the Nile in 1798, in which most of the French transport ships were sunk off Alexandria, isolated Napoleon's armies in Egypt and they were ultimately forced to leave. Napoleon was the first to go, embarking for Europe secretly, one early dawn, but he arrived safely back in France, bluffed his way through awkward explanations and once more prepared to invade England. Along our southern shores the people of England stood watch and guard for nearly five more years.

Under Pitt's persuasion, Austria, Russia, Sweden and Naples allied themselves with England against Napoleon, who now proclaimed himself Emperor of the French. Nelson's victory at Trafalgar, in 1805, removed the danger of French invasion of England and tension relaxed, but the war dragged on for another ten years. Pitt died and Lord Greville became Prime Minister.

It was not until Napoleon had been defeated in Russia, in Spain and finally at Waterloo, in 1815, that the war came to an end, and at the Congress of Vienna, during the final peace settlements, our possession of the Cape of Good Hope and Ceylon was confirmed.

For England this was the last of the Georgian wars, but at home she faced a host of social problems, with a multitude of underpaid industrial workers seething with unrest and a vast army of discharged soldiers coming home to seek employment.

The Battle of Trafalgar. Nelson was killed but England was made safe from French invasion

Chapter Two

COSTUME AND FASHION

Fashions in costume are not arbitrary whims of the designers. The changes they make reflect the changing moods and habits of the society they serve. The varying economic and social position of women affects fashion, the availability of new materials and the general affairs of the country, whether it be at peace or at war, prosperous or poor.

During the eighteenth century fashion changed slowly – more slowly in fact than one might have expected, with so many new forces at work. The difficulty of communication between country towns and the capital meant that the fashions worn in London were slow to be copied elsewhere, while the bulk of the population, too poor to consider the vagaries of fashion, continued to wear such simple and serviceable clothes as they could procure. Nevertheless, there are certain well marked characteristics of Georgian dress and these, though affected in the first place by the aristocracy, were gradually copied by the upper and middle classes and eventually, with obvious adaptations and modifications, by poorer people everywhere.

Men's Dress

When George I came to the throne, men of fashion were still wearing the long wigs of human hair which had been introduced from France by Charles II at the Restoration. These wigs had long curls hanging down behind and over each shoulder and with them men wore coats of silk, satin or velvet,

Man's town dress in early Georgian times. He wears a long, curling wig, coat and waistcoat both reaching to the knees, breeches, stockings and leather shoes, with a sword at the waist

over long waistcoats, both reaching to the knees and concealing the breeches. Brightly coloured silk stockings came up over the knees and their fine white linen shirts were frilled and trimmed with lace and beautiful lace fichus. Leather shoes were fastened with jewelled buckles and had low wooden heels. Every gentleman wore a sword and in cold weather and for travelling a long, circular cloth cloak. The hat was a large beaver tricorn but as this was difficult to perch on a curling wig it was more often carried.

In the country men wore more serviceable clothes. The coat was cut away in the front for freedom of movement, particularly when riding, and stout leather boots fitted closely to the calves.

There was no regulation dress for special occasions yet. At Court men wore the best they had. Army officers mainly wore red coats but this was also a popular colour for civilians and there was no accepted uniform yet for the navy.

The lace cravat gradually gave way to a silk cravat and coats tended to become soberer in colour, fine cloth taking the place of silk or velvet, but waistcoats were still ornate and the basic style did not change for many years.

The cumbersome wigs were obviously inconvenient and men began to tie them back and enclose them in black taffeta bags tied with a neat bow. The army set the fashion for these bag wigs but they were soon adopted by civilians. As an alternative they plaited the hair into a pigtail.

The head was closely shaved under these wigs and at home, when men discarded them along with their stiff clothes, they wore an embroidered cap or turban and a loose silk robe.

Wigs grew smaller. By the 1730's bob wigs had been designed, which looked more like natural hair. They were considerably cheaper and were worn almost universally, by

Man's dress of the mid-18th century. He wears a tricorn hat over a small wig, a shorter waistcoat, and the coat is cut away in front for easier movement

A pig-tail wig of the early 18th century

professional men and ordinary citizens, shopkeepers and app-
rentices: and with them went a smaller and plainer tricorn hat.
Wigs were always powdered for formal occasions and when
sometimes the natural hair was left in front the join between
this and the wig was concealed with powder.

By the 1750's wigs and tricorn hats were small and neat and
coats and waistcoats elegant and well cut. Even most of the
army still wore tricorns, except some of the Guards, who
adopted the mitre hat. For the next twenty years there was
little change, but gradually the fashion for wearing swords
declined, except when attending Court. In 1756, the year of
the outbreak of the Seven Years War, the first umbrella was
seen in London, carried by Jonas Hanway, but it was a long
time before anyone else followed his example.

As the century wore on the cut of the coat became simpler
but the colours brighter. Waistcoats were shorter and the front
of the coat was cut away like the riding coats, gradually
developing into the tail coat.

By about 1775 long walking sticks with gold or silver knobs
were carried, wigs became even smaller and the tricorn hat
smaller still, worn tilted forward over the brows. Coats were no
longer so elaborate and embroidered and even waistcoats were
less ornate, while shoes tended to become flat heeled.

Men grew tired of their tricorns. Some punched them
into the shape worn by Napoleon, straight across the head,
others perched them fore and aft, like the hat of a British
admiral. Towards the end of the century the tricorn disappeared for ever, to be replaced by the tall, silk hat. It was first
worn in London in 1797 by its designer, a haberdasher, and
caused such a commotion that he was charged with a breach of
the peace for having, according to the St. James's Gazette,
'appeared on the public highway wearing upon his head a tall
structure having a shining lustre and calculated to frighten
timid people. Several women had fainted at the sight, children
screamed, dogs yelped and a small boy had had his arms
broken.'

However, by about the time of Waterloo tall silk hats had safely arrived and the long reign of the beaver hat was over. They were broad brimmed at first and the crown was wider at the top than at the base.

By about the time of the French Revolution coats were double breasted with wide revers, cut short in front to show the waistcoat, and with long tails. Sleeves were narrow and long and a folded neckcloth was worn. Shoe-laces were replacing buckles though high boots were worn as often as shoes.

The advent of shoe-laces caused consternation amongst the buckle-makers and a newspaper of the time hoped that 'the fashion for shoelaces will not become prevalent, as so many shoe-buckle manufacturing families will be wiped out.' There was even an attempt to ban them, but the English genius for compromise was remarked upon by Sophie v. La Roche, when she visited London in 1786. '. . . there are men who dodge the ban upon the coming fashion of tying shoes with laces, which threatens to ruin buckle-makers,' she wrote, 'by wearing a buckle on one foot and a shoe-lace on the other.'

The craze for wigs was waning. As early as 1763 the peruke makers had been complaining that gentlemen were taking to wearing their own hair, with a resulting decline in business. By the 80's and 90's wigs were similar to those worn today by barristers, flat on top with two or three rows of curls on either side and a short queue, but the final blow to the fashion came when Pitt imposed his powder tax in 1795. Soon after that only members of the legal profession and the Church were wearing them.

By the end of the century men were wearing for town and country alike a tail coat, waistcoat and breeches of fine woollen cloth, plain but impeccably tailored, and the increasingly popular tall silk hat. Beau Brummel, for a while a friend of the Prince Regent, set the standard of English tailoring with his beautifully cut coats, and the fashionable London tailors vied with each other to secure his patronage. Before he lost all his money in the gaming clubs and sank into obscure poverty,

*Man's dress of the 1830's.
He is wearing tight trousers,
a plain jacket over a neatly
buttoned waistcoat and a
top hat*

Brummel's impeccable clothes, snuff boxes and canes were the talk of the town. It was he who first thought of starching the cravat and the Mirror of May 7th, 1825, reporting this latest fashion, said that at the sight of it 'dandies were struck dumb with envy and washerwomen miscarried.'

Early in the nineteenth century trousers began to be worn instead of breeches, either tapering to a tight fit round the ankle or strapped under the instep of the boots. Within a few years they were universal. Men also took to heavy overcoats for cold weather with a series of overlapping capes.

For a while the dandies wore their coat collars so high that they brushed their cheeks. Their chests were padded and also their hips, under their skin-tight trousers. But this was the Englishman's last sartorial fling for many years to come. By the 1830's England's industrialisation was well under way, and though men still let their fancy roam when choosing the colour of their waistcoats, there was a growing fashion for dark and sombre colours, which was to remain for another hundred years or more.

Women's Dress

At the beginning of Georgian times women's dress was very attractive, with a low-cut stiff bodice, loose, elbow-length sleeves, trimmed with deep ruffles of lace, and a long full skirt, opened in front and draped back in folds over side panniers, to show a flowered petticoat. The curious high lace headdress of Queen Anne's time was still fashionable but by 1720 it had disappeared, and for the next fifty years women wore their hair neatly pinned close to the head and surmounted by a small lace cap.

Before long, however, the side panniers were replaced by circular hoops which, with the passing years, grew ever larger. The hoop was a petticoat stiffened with whale bone, and whale bone was also used to stiffen the corset, which was as formidable as ever, laced at the back and reinforced with a stout wire round the top. With the arrival of the hoop women were able to discard some of their cumbersome petticoats, which had been worn to give fullness to the skirt. Some dispensed with them altogether and as knickers had not yet been devised they wore nothing under their hoops but gartered stockings and a plain linen shift, worn underneath the corset. Scotch and Irish linen were available but were rather coarse. The finest linen at this time, but a good deal more expensive, came from Holland. No one had yet thought of silk or lace for underclothes.

Wealthy women wore dresses of rich silks, damasks and brocades, but with the arrival of the thinner silks, muslins and cottons from the East they seem, regardless of the rigours of the English climate, to have preferred them. They were certainly a great deal lighter than the richer stuffs for their voluminous skirts, which took yards of material, and cotton was sometimes quilted with wadding, which must have been a great comfort at times.

Inevitably English cloth makers protested about the increasing use of imported fabrics and laws were passed at one time to forbid them, but they were henceforth smuggled into the country in such large quantities that it made little difference and fashion prevailed.

Up till the 1730's stockings of all colours were worn, green being particularly popular, but after this time there was a craze for white stockings, either of silk, worsted or thread, which lasted till the end of the century. Shoes were high-heeled and rather clumsy, with the heel too far under the instep for comfortable walking, so women wore slippers in the house. Pattens and overshoes afforded some protection from muddy roads but Mrs Purefroy, writing from Buckingham in 1735, complained that 'every place is now so deep in dirt where one walks that my Galloshoes are of no service to me.'

Out of doors, women wore cloaks and hoods. In the early part of the century these were invariably scarlet, like Red Riding Hood's, but later they were more often black.

As the hooped skirt grew larger, nearly every woman took to it, including country women and servants. But the circular hoop was monstrously inconvenient. In the narrow streets two women could hardly pass each other. Some time during the 1740's a more manageable oval hoop was designed but this was the only important change in fashion for some years.

By the middle of the century women were wearing 'milk-maid' straw hats, tied with ribbons over their lace caps, and their dresses were of delicate lawns, muslins and flower printed cottons. The oval hoops were a little smaller by now but corsets were as tight as ever. Dresses were longer-waisted and sometimes laced in front over a stomacher, but elbow-length, ruffle-trimmed sleeves were still worn and bodices were still low cut. Fichus or small capes were sometimes worn over the bodices and winter cloaks and hoods were warm and comfortable.

After 1763 English women were visiting Paris again and French milliners and dressmakers arrived in London. One of

Woman's dress of the 1740's. The dress is draped over a wide oval hoop. She wears a lace cap and carries a straw hat which is tied on with ribbons

the most useful fashions they brought with them was an adjustable farthingale, which could be raised on either side when passing in and out of doorways or getting into a carriage. They also introduced a new hairdressing style. English women abandoned their simple hairdressing and now took to building their hair high on top of the head. In the 1770's came the full force of the new fashion. Women took to wearing headdresses so large that they soon became monstrous. Their own hair was frizzed over large wire frames and any deficiencies were filled in with wool. The whole erection was well greased, then dusted with grey or white powder, and decorated with feathers and flowers. Hannah More, during her early years in London, wrote of young women who had on their heads 'an acre and a half of shrubbery besides slopes, garden plots, tulip beds, clumps of peonies, kitchen gardens and greenhouses.'

The craze lasted for several years, for when Sophie visited

During the 1770's women of fashion took to wearing these high and complicated headdresses

A fashion of the late 1770's. This was the 'sack' dress, tightly fitting in front but at the back hanging from the shoulders in loose pleats to a short train

the Haymarket Theatre in 1786 four ladies entered a box 'with such wonderfully fantastic caps and hats perched on their heads, that they were received by the entire audience with loud derision . . . and when the expression of the remarks became too strong, they . . . departed.' Even in the nineties, when Elizabeth Fry, as a young girl, went to the play at Covent Garden, she wrote that 'my hair was dressed and I felt like a monkey.'

All women now wore hats or caps when out of doors and one of Sophie's first tasks on reaching London was to equip herself properly, for, she wrote: 'Women here may not go out without a hat. So this land with the greatest freedom of thought and creed and custom is yet in some measure fettered by convention.'

As the century wore on women occasionally took to carrying long walking sticks, like their menfolk, but the dress remained essentially the same. In the late 70's there had been a brief fashion for the 'sack dress', in which the front remained tightly fitting but the back hung down from the neck in loose pleats to a short full train. The overskirt was sometimes puffed out with crumpled paper, which made a disconcerting rustling noise, and at one time these panniered skirts became short enough to show the ankle, but by the 1780's the pannier and farthingale were going out of fashion. At first they were replaced by pads on each hip and later by a single pad placed in the small of the back. Then skirts dropped down to the ground again.

Some country gentlewomen adopted a practical and rather masculine type of dress. Though the skirt was long and full it was very plain and with it they wore a jacket cut like a man's riding jacket and a man's beaver hat and more comfortable walking shoes.

Headdresses grew smaller, though they were still rather high and elaborate, and mob caps, which were useful to cover the hair when it was not properly curled and dressed, were very large indeed, looking more like rather ungainly hoods than the caps of earlier years.

With the French Revolution and its aftermath, women's fashions in France changed startingly. Women discarded their silks, satins and brocades, and influenced by Napoleon's campaign in the eastern Mediterranean and Egypt, they adopted a pseudo-classical style, like the women's dress depicted on Greek frescoes and vases. French women now put away their corsets and wore dresses made of the flimsiest white muslin,

The Empire style of the early nineteenth century, high-waisted, with short, puffed sleeves

very plain and full, confined by a single ribbon tied high under the breasts. These dresses were barely decent, for they were transparent and underneath the wearers sometimes wore nothing but pink tights.

Before long the fashion had reached England. Few English women went to the extremes of the French for long – though long enough for the newspapers to point out the dangers of being caught out in the rain in such outfits. Nevertheless, the high-waisted dress made of the flimsiest materials, and nearly always white, remained fashionable in England for the next twenty years, and well into the nineteenth century. Women discarded their corsets and braved the weather in a way which seems quite inexplicable.

Their dresses were made of English cottons and muslins now, so it was the turn of the East India Company to complain of loss of business. To compensate for their scanty dresses, they took to cashmere shawls and fichus, large fur muffs and short fitted coats, known as 'spencers'. As there was no possibility of making a useful pocket in a muslin dress, reticules were designed which, as handbags, women have used ever since. In place of high heeled shoes, they now wore flat slippers, made of satin for the evening and morocco leather for daytime.

Caps lost favour and women took to classical looking bandeaux for evening, which were often made of strips of coloured embroidery. Some, still under the eastern influence, took to turbans, which for important evening functions were ornamented with ostrich feathers, the higher and straighter the better, though no one exceeded the Duchess of Devonshire, who on one occasion managed to find a feather which was four feet high.

By early in the nineteenth century women had grown tired of their flimsy, one-piece dresses and took to wearing an over-tunic with puffed sleeves. In every way, clothes became more feminine. Dresses though still high waisted and made of flimsy materials, were more complicated. Stays came back and the poke bonnet appeared, together with plaid scarves and shawls, ankle boots, furs and heavier cloaks. It was about this time that long, tight-fitting and lace-trimmed drawers were designed for women and by the 1830's they were worn universally.

White was still fashionable, especially for evening dress and ball gowns, but more colours were worn now, particularly pink, blue, lilac and pale yellow.

Skirts were growing wider and hems were stiffened. The waist went back to its normal place and during the 1830's the bodice was long and very tight at the waist, with often a heart-shaped neckline. Velvet and poplin were coming into favour and the wide skirt came down to just above the ankles. Sleeves were very full and sometimes puffed out with wicker frames or small feather cushions. White silk stockings were now very fine, for those who could afford them, but they were always worn over flesh-coloured cashmere ones.

English women were becoming soberer and less romantic in their dress and at the same time a good deal warmer. By the time the young Queen Victoria came to the throne lace fichus had given place to plain velvet or watered silk collars. Sleeves were tight, bodices plain and skirts becoming heavier and longer. Shawls were worn at all times of the year – cashmere in winter and lace or net in summer. The hair was dressed lower, with demure curls hanging against each cheek. Nearly all women wore poke bonnets, with the brim pulled down on either side so that it almost encircled the face. Black silk mittens were fashionable and flat-heeled, square-toed shoes.

During the early part of the 18th century children were dressed very like their parents, when they were still very young

Children's Dress

During the eighteenth century new born babies were still closely swaddled with cotton bandages, over which they were dressed in linen or lawn petticoats and dresses, with caps and mittens. The tight, swaddling bands were discarded towards the end of the century but throughout the nineteenth century babies were still partly bound and wore a number of long petticoats, with an elaborately embroidered long dress and shawl. During their first few years they were put into ankle-length frocks.

From the time they were free of their baby dresses, at the age of four or five, eighteenth century children were dressed very much like adults. Boys were breeched and wore a coat, waistcoat and elaborate shirt and even, sometimes, a wig, though more usually their own hair was grown long and dressed like a wig. Little girls were put into hoops and stays and long frocks.

Towards the end of the century, children's dress became less formal. Boys went into long loose trousers even before they became usual for men. They reached to between the knee and the ankle and were buttoned on to a comfortable loose blouse with an open neck and collar. Girls wore straight, high-waisted muslin dresses reaching to the ground, usually of white, but sometimes flowered, with short sleeves and a sash.

However, round about the 1830's, as women's fashion grew more formal, so did that of the children. Their days of comfort were short-lived. Boys clothes were tighter. The trousers were long, the jacket short and close-fitting, the shirt neck high and tight. Sometimes they wore tall silk hats, sometimes peaked caps, which made them look like page boys. The uniform of the modern page boy is, in fact, a survival of this fashion, and it was about this time that the style of short coat, long trousers and tall silk hat was adopted as the school uniform at Eton.

Little girls were put into layers of petticoats and full skirts, which were now only calf length, but below them showed long, frilly pantalettes. These pantalettes were a combination-like garment with legs reaching to the ankles. In winter they wore a coat with a deep cape collar, a bonnet, fur muff and gloves.

Children of the 1830's. The boy has long trousers and a short, tight-fitting jacket, the girl a full, calf-length dress worn over many petticoats and frilled pantalettes

Chapter Three

BUILDINGS

Throughout the eighteenth century, as industry, overseas commerce and large scale agriculture brought mounting profits, the rich grew richer, and they put much of their money into land, for ownership of land was still a sign of social distinction. With increasing enclosures, as land was put to more intensive cultivation, its value rose. Common lands grew scarce and the ordinary labourer was in time forced either to work on a richer man's farms and estates or seek his livelihood in a town. Once more wealth was concentrated in the hands of a relatively few rich families, who also wielded the political power. They owned vast tracts of land, sometimes nearly whole counties, as was the case of the Marlboroughs, who at one time owned nearly the whole of Oxfordshire.

Not only did they transform their own homes into palatial mansions, but they went in for speculative building, particularly in the towns, building houses for the prosperous upper and middle classes, for which they received large rent rolls. The Russell family built the houses round Covent Garden in Jacobean times, and later and through the early years of the eighteenth century they built Bloomsbury, in the fields surrounding Bedford House.

It was Inigo Jones who, in the seventeenth century, had been mainly responsible for introducing the Italian style of architecture to England. As a young man he had visited Italy and was greatly influenced by the work of the Italian architect Palladio, who had adopted a style derived from the buildings of Classical Rome. After Inigo Jones's death, Christopher Wren carried on this tradition, brilliantly adapting it to the needs of a northern climate and the materials which were available in England.

Through Wren's work and influence, the typical Queen Anne house was being built by the beginning of the eighteenth century in place of the half-timbered Tudor and early Jacobean houses. The first sash windows had been introduced and, to save space, town houses were built adjoining each other, in terraces.

The Palladian tradition in architecture was to continue for the next hundred years, in both private and public buildings, apart from a few digressions into the Baroque and Gothic styles.

The Baroque was an unconventional combination of a number of styles, adapted by the architect for the effect he wished to create. The most notable private dwelling in this style was the vast, Italianate Blenheim Palace, designed by Sir John Vanbrugh and Nicholas Hawksmoor, and intended to outshine the splendour of Versailles. Hawksmoor as a young man had helped Christopher Wren in the rebuilding of many of the City churches, as well as the hospitals at Greenwich and Chelsea, and after Wren's death he built many more London churches for the growing population, including Christ Church, Spitalfields, St. Ann's, Limehouse, St. George's, Bloomsbury – for the Russell's housing development – and St. Mary's, Woolnoth, where John Newton was to become vicar and make his plea for the emancipation of the slaves.

The reaction of a few architects to revive the Gothic style of building, with battlements and arches, was short-lived, but during the 1750's Horace Walpole, flouting fashion, built his 'little Gothic castle' at Strawberry Hill, Twickenham.

Generally speaking, after the death of Vanbrugh and Hawksmoor, architects adopted the Palladian tradition. Palladio's famous work on architecture, first published in Italy during the seventeenth century, was studied carefully

Horace Walpole's 'little Gothic castle', built at Strawberry Hill, Twickenham in the 1750's

and followed by most British architects of the later part of the eighteenth century, together with the books of Colin Campbell, who rebuilt Burlington House in Piccadilly for Lord Burlington, William Kent, who helped with the interior decorations and James Gibbs, who designed St. Martin-in-the-Fields and the Radcliffe library at Oxford.

The basic constructions of the great mansions were on similar lines, with a central block, approached by an impressive pillared portico, containing the main reception rooms, the stables in one wing and the kitchen quarters in the other, with accommodation for the servants, both connected to the main block by a colonnade. Woburn Abbey was re-built in this style during the 1750's, the new Georgian mansion being built round the earlier Jacobean house. The Oxford family rebuilt Welbeck Abbey and Viscount Palmerston part of Broadlands. Colin Campbell, as well as adding the pillared portico to Burlington House, built Houghton Hall for Sir Robert Walpole. William Kent designed Holkham Hall in Norfolk for Thomas Coke, Earl of Leicester, and George III bought Buckingham House from the Buckingham family and moved there from St. James's Palace with Queen Charlotte. Later he made it over to her and for some time it was known as the Queen's House, until George IV transformed it into Buckingham Palace.

For these noble Palladian mansions magnificent gardens and private parks were designed. Broad avenues of tall trees, sometimes several miles long, were planted to create sweeping vistas. If the ground were too flat, armies of labourers were set to work to make gently rising hills and valleys. Artificial lakes were built, temples, grottoes, bridges, obelisks and groups of statuary, in order to make a perfectly balanced scene.

This new taste for grandiose landscape gardening was introduced by William Kent and followed enthusiastically by his pupil, Capability Brown, who became the royal gardener at Hampton Court. Brown, with his craving for effects, often adopted the most extraordinary artifices, such as planting a dead tree to make a landscape more 'naturalistic', building artificial ruins to give balance to a vista, and was even guilty of making fake bridges, such as the one to be found in the gardens of Kenwood, Hampstead Heath.

Town Houses

The population of England was growing. Cities such as Norwich, Bristol and Bath were spreading, but faster than any of them was the growth of London. To economise space and preserve dignity, terraces of houses were built for the well-to-do, both the gentry and the prosperous middle-classes. In London these houses were built of brick, in stone districts such as Bath of the local stone. The dividing walls were thick, as a precaution against fire spreading from one house to the next, and these party walls also carried the chimney stacks. Usually they were four stories high, approached by a short flight of steps, with the principal rooms on the first floor and the kitchen premises hidden away in a basement, which was approached by a steep flight of steps running down from the pavement to an area, protected and hidden by iron railings.

A crescent house at Bath, built of Bath stone, in the mid-18th century

Sash windows were always used in these new houses. On the ground floor they were relatively small, tall and impressive on the first floor where the important rooms were situated, shorter on the floor above and completely square on the top floor.

The front door was imposing, flanked by pillars and surmounted by a semi-circular fanlight. The entrance hall was wide and from it led a spiral stone staircase, balustraded in wrought iron.

The oak panelling of the old days gave way to plastered walls and moulded ceilings. Doorways and fireplaces were elaborate architectural creations. Doors were flanked by pillars and often surmounted by triangular pediments and decorative moulding, and the fireplaces were similarly elaborate.

These houses were built sometimes in straight rows, as in Harley Street, sometimes in beautiful crescents, as at Bath – many of which were built by the architect Wood and his son – and sometimes in squares, surrounding gardens of trees and shrubs, as in Bloomsbury.

During the reign of George III the fashionable architects were the Adam brothers. Robert Adam, the eldest of the four, had travelled widely. His first important work was the building of the Adelphi terrace on the Thames Embankment, the form of which had been suggested to him after visiting Diocletian's palace at Spalato. This work was begun in 1768 and Robert Adam imported hundreds of Irish labourers, at a low rate of pay, to complete it.

He built Kenwood at Hampstead Heath and also Luton Hoo, but as well as these mansions he and his brothers built many terraced houses in London, in the Palladian tradition. Portland Place is an outstanding example of their work as well as parts of Fitzroy Square and many streets of much smaller houses, including those running up from the Embankment to the Strand, whose names show their origin, John Street and Adam Street.

The Adam houses did not differ in essentials from those of the earlier terraced houses. This was the style which satisfied the taste of the age and it was maintained almost rigidly for many years. It was fortunate that the standard set by the wealthy was, in fact, so elegant, for it meant that the less prosperous, who copied them, lived in houses of similar grace.

The distinction of the Adam houses lay in their detail and style of decoration, the inspiration for which was pure Greek. Doorways were particularly attractive, the fanlights being of the most beautifully delicate designs, the glass panels making up the pattern being joined together with bars of fine lead. Banisters of the staircase were of beautifully wrought iron with mahogany handrails, and they also added wrought-iron balconies to some of their houses. Ceilings were of plaster work and the marble fireplaces were carved with Greek motifs such as urns, swags of drapery and garlands of flowers.

Leverton was another architect working at the same time as the Adams and following the same tradition. Quite small houses were now being built in this style and the flat, plain plastered walls of the rooms were sometimes coloured in pale greens, blues, lilac, grey or primrose yellow, all of which looked particularly attractive against the mahogany doors.

During the 1760's Chinese hand-painted wall papers were being imported and the interest in Chinese art and decoration was stimulated after Sir William Chambers' visit to China and the appearance of his book on Chinese art. On his return he built the pagoda at Kew Gardens, but his most important piece of work was probably the rebuilding of Somerset House, in the Palladian style, round about 1776. And about this time, George Dance, the son of the architect who had built the Mansion House, built Newgate prison.

Regency Building

During the Regency and the reign of George IV the classical tradition was maintained in the building of new houses for the upper and middle classes. They were built either singly or in terraces and the bricks were very often covered with stucco or plaster, a fashion imported from Italy.

John Nash was the fashionable and important architect of the Regency period. English architectural standards had never been higher and he and his followers continued to build in the classical style, adding a few Gothic, Oriental and Egyptian

A marble fireplace, carved with a pattern of Greek urns and garlands of flowers. Designed by Adam

decorative motifs. Terraces of smaller houses were almost fragile looking, with their delicate ironwork balconies, to which were added metal roofs curved like Chinese pagodas. Windows were tall and narrow, with very thin glazing bars. Bay windows appeared, often with semi-circular ironwork balconies on the first floors and curving metal roofs. Ground floor windows sometimes had curved tops to match the semicircular fanlights over the front doors. At the back, curving stone steps often led from a balcony to the garden. Many of these charming little houses have fortunately survived, particularly in places such as Cheltenham and Brighton.

In London the Regency building was on a grandiose scale. In 1811 several hundreds of acres of land north of the Marylebone Road reverted to the crown and the Prince Regent asked Nash to develop them as a fashionable residential area. Nash planned a garden city of imposing terraces of Palladian mansions, surrounding a park which was re-named Regent's Park. The terraces were magnificent, Cumberland Terrace perhaps the grandest of them all. Many had private carriage ways, approached by triumphal arches. And they were all, including the villas standing in their own grounds, which he built between the terraces, of brick covered with gleaming white stucco.

Regent Street and the Quadrant, built by John Nash between 1817 and 1823. The colonnades were removed in 1848

Many of the army of workmen were unemployed soldiers back from the Napoleonic wars and Nash has been accused of allowing careless and slipshod workmanship behind his gorgeous facades, but fundamentally the houses were sound. They were well ventilated and the heating and plumbing arrangements were of the most recent design then known.

Nash planned to link Regent's Park with St. James's Park and built Regent Street with its beautiful quadrant between 1817 and 1823. The following year he designed the charming little church of All Soul's, Langham Place.

He planned to rebuild the area south of Regent Street and cut a way through to Bloomsbury from a large square at the top of Whitehall, which in the 1830's was to become Trafalgar Square. Many of his plans were never completed but a number of the tumbledown buildings surrounding St. Martin-in-the-Fields were rebuilt about this time by Cubitt, Wilkins and Smirke.

After George III died and the Regent became George IV, Carlton House was pulled down and Nash designed Carlton

House Terrace on the site. He also transformed Buckingham House – the Queen's House – into Buckingham Palace for the new king.

Other notable buildings of the early nineteenth century in London were Sir John Soane's Bank of England and Smirke's British Museum.

Brighton

Sea bathing was becoming popular in the later part of the eighteenth century and after a first visit to Brighton in 1783 the young prince who was to become Prince Regent bought a farmhouse in this little fishing village for a summer residence. A few years later, after his secret marriage to Maria Fitzherbert, he commissioned Henry Holland to transform the farmhouse into a small, classical villa.

Throughout the following years many additions were made to the Prince's seaside pavilion, including some of the increasingly popular bamboo and lacquer furnishings and porcelain vases and some very beautiful, hand-painted Chinese wall papers.

Then, in 1815, a few years after he had assumed the Regency, he commissioned John Nash to transform the whole of the exterior of the pavilion into an Eastern palace. Before the wondering eyes of the people of Brighton there arose Nash's astonishing but strangely beautiful pavilion, with its Indian

The Royal Pavilion, Brighton, rebuilt for the Prince Regent by John Nash, in 1815, with Indian minarets, domes and pinnacles

Royal Adelaide Crescent, Hove, built during the 1830's, partly by Decimus Burton

minarets, domes and pinnacles. Two new state apartments were also added, the banqueting room and the music room.

Fashion followed the Prince Regent to Brighton and it was round about this time that many of the magnificent terraces and crescents were built, as, for example, Sussex Square and Lewes Crescent. Royal Adelaide Crescent in Hove, with its pillared porches surmounted by square balconies, very similar to houses in Kensington and Pimlico, was partly the work of Decimus Burton, and though it was begun in the last year of George IV's reign it was not finished till William IV was on the throne and it was named after his queen.

The charming extravagancies of the Regency buildings were the last graces of a way of life which was to change abruptly. The grey shadows of the Industrial Revolution were spreading over the countryside and bringing an outcrop of industrial buildings and sordid little industrial cottages for the increasing millions of workers, with desperate medieval revivals for those who were trying to escape from the tidal wave of technological and mechanical progress.

Chapter Four

IN THE HOME

Furniture

At the beginning of Georgian times walnut veneer on beech, or some similar, relatively inexpensive wood, was used for the better kinds of furniture, though solid oak was still used in country districts. Early in the eighteenth century the first pieces of mahogany were imported from the West Indies. Mahogany, or Spanish mahogany as it was called, was hard, heavy and reliable. It soon became more popular than walnut and was imported in increasing quantities from the West Indies, till it was used almost exclusively for many years. The first mahogany pieces were polished with linseed oil. Then the technique of polishing with brickdust, applied with a cork, was introduced and later still the wood was varnished.

Early Georgian mahogany cupboard

Walnut furniture had always been veneered, except for the legs of chairs, which were of solid walnut, but mahogany was used in the solid throughout the whole piece. One of the most useful pieces of furniture made during the first half of the eighteenth century was the mahogany press. The upper part was a cupboard, fitted with oak trays, which slid forward on runners. The lower part was a chest of drawers comprising two adjacent small drawers above two long ones. The doors were panelled, as the old solid oak furniture had been, and the drawers were surrounded with a narrow beading, which helped to keep out dust.

Chairs

The shape of chairs did not alter greatly. The winged and upholstered armchair with curved arms of Queen Anne's time was still made but the cabriole legs, now of mahogany, were often elaborately carved at the knees and feet, characteristic motifs being a mask or elaborate pattern of acanthus leaves on the knee, a lion's head with paw feet or an eagle's head with claw feet. In less costly chairs the claw and ball of Queen Anne's period was still popular but the more ornately carved legs were characteristic of the Georgian work.

In upright chairs with upholstered seats the rounded back of earlier times became straighter, with a straight top rail, and the back splat was carved in an openwork, fretted pattern.

Side Tables

Sideboards were not yet made but there were plenty of side tables in both dining rooms and drawing rooms. These were often marble-topped, with elaborate mahogany cabriole legs.

During the reign of George I William Kent designed furniture to fit his Palladian houses, including marble topped tables with elaborately carved and heavily gilded legs.

In time the side table or console table was often built against a wall, as a permanent fixture, needing therefore no back legs.

*Tapestry upholstered
armchair. Early 18th
century*

It was usually surmounted by a wall mirror, often in an elaborately carved and gilded frame, and flanked by candle stands.

Dining Tables

English mahogany dining tables developed from the earlier gate-legged tables, two of the legs moving out on hinges to support the extensions. They were either rectangular or circular.

Throughout the first half of the eighteenth century there were no striking developments in furniture design. The cabinet makers were turning out pieces very much in the Queen Anne style which were of impeccable workmanship, and mahogany was now used almost exclusively.

Chippendale

The new developments came about 1745. Chippendale, a brilliant master cabinet maker, opened workshops first in Long Acre and then, in 1753, in St Martin's Lane. The following year he published a trade catalogue *The Gentleman and Cabinet Maker's Directory*, which contained many furniture designs, some new, some already in use, with directions for making them.

The furniture from Chippendale's workshops and from other cabinet makers who used his book became immensely popular and the Chippendale period of furniture had begun.

Chairs

The armchair with padded seat and mahogany arms, back and legs still owed much to the Queen Anne period, but the cabriole legs were lighter and the knees higher, so that the chair did not look too bow-legged. They were often carved with acanthus leaves and finished with a simple turned club foot. The back was only slightly curved and the top rail straight, the splat being carved and pierced.

Chairs without arms were similar but stretcher rails were introduced again and legs were sometimes completely plain or very simply moulded, and square in section.

In the country, cabinet makers made similar but cheaper chairs, sometimes in mahogany but also in beech or oak which was stained to look like mahogany. They also made the first ladder-back chairs.

Chinese Chippendale

The interest in Chinese art and design was reflected in furniture design for a few years. It did not affect the basic design but decorative Chinese motifs were introduced and delicate lattice work carving. This style has come to be known as 'Chinese Chippendale' and went with the fashion for Chinese wall paper, porcelain and hangings. There was also a passing fancy for Gothic motifs in decoration and Gothic arches and groups of columns appeared occasionally on chairs, tables and cabinets.

Armchairs

An armchair with no wings was designed. The upholstered back was plain with an almost straight top, the arms gently scrolled and the seat square and plain. The mahogany legs were straight, plain and square, with plain stretcher rails.

*Mahogany chairs in
the style of
Chippendale.
Mid-18th century*

Settees

The upholstered winged settee with a high back and cabriole legs was still made. Another form had a padded seat but the back and arms were of mahogany, the splats of the back being elaborately fretted.

Tables

Chippendale re-introduced veneering for tables. It was thicker than the walnut veneer, being about an eighth of an inch, and he sometimes glued three or four layers of veneer together for extra strength. The small side table for the dining room was as simple and elegant as the dining table itself. He also made many different types of occasional tables, including a circular-topped table with a piecrust edging, supported on three cabriole legs, often carved in a pattern of acanthus leaves. From the 1760's onwards small circular tables were made, supported by three cabriole legs fixed to a vertical pillar. Sometimes they had a small gallery of turned spindles round the edge.

When a hostess was dispensing tea, one of these tables would be placed beside each guest for the tea cup. They were also used for wine glasses and are sometimes known as 'wine tables'.

*Mahogany occasional
table with 'pie-crust'
edge, in the style of
Chippendale.
Mid-18th century*

Bureaux and Writing Tables

A few secretaires were made. When they were closed they looked like a clothes chest or small press but there was an upright flap in front which could be pulled down to form a writing table. Bureaux with bookcases above, enclosed by glass doors, were more popular. The glass doors were very attractive, the glass panels fitted into bars of mahogany moulding to form a variety of simple geometric patterns. These bureaux rested either on bracket feet or a solid plinth.

Corner cupboards with similar glass doors, for the display of china and porcelain, were also popular.

Plain kneehole writing desks were made and when they were of solid mahogany they were beautifully carved.

The Bedroom

The press and the chest of drawers were to be found in most well-to-do bedrooms by now. The less pretentious were solid mahogany or mahogany veneer, plain and attractively simple, with four large useful drawers, brass drop handles and bracket feet.

For those who could afford them, there were more elaborate chests of drawers, the designs for which were taken from French models. These commodes were made in England of

solid mahogany and both front and sides had a double or
serpentine curve. They usually had three long drawers and
rested on carved and elaborately scrolled legs. The handles and
other decorations were rather florid, in the French rococo style
of Louis XIV and XV.

Dressing Tables

Dressing tables looked like plain cabinets when they were
closed. The top opened outwards from the middle to form two
projecting leaves and inside was a mirror which could be
pulled upright and various small compartments for bottles and
boxes. These little tables were fitted with a drawer and sometimes small recessed cupboards below.

Beds

Four-poster beds were lighter and made of mahogany. During
the Chinese craze a few were made with a pagoda-shaped
canopy but generally speaking they were becoming less
elaborate and cumbersome, the curtains lighter and less
voluminous.

The four poster lasted through much of the nineteenth century but towards the end of the eighteenth century the tent bed
was also used, in which the curtains hung from a light, iron
framework, and they were, of course, a good deal cheaper than
the mahogany four posters, with their carved canopies and
posts.

Clocks

The mahogany grandfather clocks of the Chippendale style
had a characteristic pediment of a double scroll above the
rounded top of the clock case door.

Hepplewhite

A few years after Chippendale had opened his workshops in
St Martin's Lane and was at the height of his popularity,
Hepplewhite, another cabinet maker, opened his business in

Cripplegate. He, too, wrote a catalogue, *The Cabinet Maker and Upholsterer's Guide,* though it was not published until 1786, two years after his death.

Hepplewhite's furniture was generally rather simpler than Chippendale's though equally elegant, and his individual style was marked by new types of decoration. He introduced painting and gilding and also inlay of bands of satinwood, rosewood and ebony. In his carving he used classical motifs, such as vases, swags of draped cloth and husks.

Chairs with serpentine top rails and shield or heart-shaped backs, or backs which are in the form of hoops or ovals, all belong to the Hepplewhite school of design, which many cabinet makers adopted. Mahogany sidetables, writing tables, bureaux, chests of drawers, tallboys and wardrobes or presses were all restrained and graceful and very like the work of the Sheraton school which was to follow a few years later.

Adam

Unlike Chippendale and Hepplewhite, Robert Adam was a designer of furniture who passed his drawings on to a practical cabinet maker. Primarily an architect, he designed delicate furniture to match the style of decoration of his rooms and some of it was made in the Chippendale workshops. Many other cabinet makers were to copy his designs and Adam furniture became a distinctive style. Adam was responsible for the first sideboard as we know it today. About 1780 he made pedestal cupboards to stand on either side of the side table, fitted with plate warmers and wine bins, and surmounted by large classical Greek urns of zinc-lined mahogany for storing cutlery: and in time these three pieces, with the urns, were constructed as one composite piece of furniture.

Adam carving was always in classical motifs, delicate acanthus leaves, the Greek honeysuckle, chains of husks, the Greek key pattern, vases, drapery and plaques carved with subjects from Greek mythology. He sometimes used inlay and occasionally marquetry, with decorative woods such as satin-

A mahogany chair with shield-shaped back in the Hepplewhite style. About 1780

wood, tulip wood and rosewood. He did not use cabriole legs, preferring the square, tapered leg with a small square foot: and towards the end of the eighteenth century the cabriole leg went completely out of fashion. Some of his furniture was painted with floral sprays on a cream or pale green ground, in the style of Angelica Kauffman. Angelica was living in London during the late sixties and throughout the seventies and she was one of the artists Adam employed to decorate the main rooms of some of the mansions he designed, including Ken House, Chandos House, Luton Hoo and Harewood House, as well as some of the Adelphi houses.

Sheraton

Thomas Sheraton was the last of the eighteenth century cabinet makers. He arived in London from the North of England in 1790 and a year or two later published *The Cabinet Maker and Upholsterer's Drawing Book,* which again provided furniture designs and instructions for making them. Sheraton's work was in many ways similar to that of Hepplewhite but his chairs were notably lighter. The backs of his upright chairs were lower, horizontal bars replaced the vertical splat, and the top rail was a separate piece of construction. The arm-pieces of his armchairs did not splay out but rose with the back in a continuing gentle curve.

57

Sheraton sometimes painted his furniture, using the floral motifs and panels made popular by Angelica Kauffmann, and he also used inlay, but not a great deal of carving. Towards the end of the century he introduced a bow-fronted sideboard.

He made long mirrors swinging on a footed support, known as 'horse' glasses and later as cheval glasses, and also small, vase-shaped mirrors swinging on curved supports, the stand being bow-fronted and fitted with a small drawer.

The 'chaise longue' was very popular in the early years of the nineteenth century, taking the place of the seventeenth and eighteenth century day beds. Adam had adapted it from a French design and the 'Madame Recamier' couch was very similar to the one in David's picture, with deeply scrolled head and foot, the legs curving outwards to continue the line and the small feet often fitted with casters.

The low sofa table was a useful accompaniment to the chaise longue. These tables were adapted from the Pembroke table of the 1760's to 1780's, the side flaps supported by fly brackets and the square legs often finished with casters. Many were decorated with the most beautiful marquetry and some were also games tables, having a central panel chequered in contrasting woods for draughts and chess. The table had pierced insets for marking the score for cribbage and the panel slid away to reveal a recess marked out for a form of backgammon known as tric-trac.

In drawing rooms furnished with such elegance the teapoy was usually found. The hostess always brewed her tea in front of her guests and the tea caddy stood on a small table by her side. About 1810 a cabinet maker designed a caddy and table as a single piece of furniture, called a teapoy, which was often decorated to match the sofa table, with wonderful rosewood or satinwood maquetry on mahogany.

Papier maché was introduced about this time, particularly for chairs, but it was used much more a little later in the century, during the early years of Queen Victoria.

In country districts the Chippendale, Hepplewhite and Sheraton designs were sometimes copied by local carpenters in chestnut, elm or yew but the useful oak dresser of Tudor times was still made and the simple wheel-back chair became very popular, the finest specimens being made in Norfolk and Suffolk.

Wallpaper

In early Georgian times the walls of wealthy houses were covered with oak panelling, tapestry, silk, damask or velvet. Smaller and newer houses had either plain, plastered walls or walls covered with wainscotting of painted deal, which was a good deal more economical than oak. Chinese and other hand-painted wall papers were very expensive but by the middle of the eighteenth century wallpapers were being printed and became very popular.

In Walpole's Gothic villa at Twickenham he had a straw coloured paper printed with 'Gothic detail', a blue and white striped paper adorned with festoons, and in his bedroom a deep purple paper.

Curtains

The large windows of both town and country mansions were draped with elaborately fringed pelmets and curtains, and even in less pretentious homes windows were dressed with muslin

A little girl's sampler.
18th century

curtains and heavy silk or serge outer curtains, often trimmed with bobble fringe.

Mrs Purefroy wrote to London for '18 yards of chintz to make window curtains' for a drawing room, or something 'that would suit workt chairs, workt in shades upon white . . .' She also used Indian damask and sprigged calico for window curtains.

Carpets

Oriental rugs and carpets were imported and English worked needlework carpets were used. Towards the end of the eighteenth century carpets were being manufactured in England.

Needlework

Tapestry work in wool and silk was as popular during the eighteenth century as in Stuart times and was used to cover chairs, settees, fire-screens and stools and also for carpets.

Early in the century mainly floral paterns were used, though the leaves and flowers were less stylised than in the Jacobean work. To upholster the furniture of the famous cabinet makers a great deal of beautiful needlework was done, still using naturalistic flowers but sometimes introducing classical motifs as well, particularly vases. Human figures were occasionally worked, reminiscent of those introduced by the French weavers in the Cluny and Gobelins looms.

French hand tapestry work at this time was of extreme delicacy and the designs were copied by English embroideresses. They were mainly floral, sometimes with stylised leaves curving into long scrolls which outlined the whole pattern, sometimes, as in the old French brocade patterns, arranged in bands of tiny flower sprays on alternating background colours, to produce the stripes which Hepplewhite admired so much.

Another style of needlework for upholstery was Florentine work, in which a repeating pattern of a geometric shape – the Vandyke, oyster, melon or fleur-de-lis – completely covered the canvas.

Hooded range and mechanical spits in the kitchen of the Royal Pavilion, Brighton

Kitchen and Cooking

During most of the eighteenth century cooking was done on an open fire. The magnificent kitchen in the Royal Pavilion at Brighton had an open fire with a large copper hood and an elaborate arrangement of mechanically revolving spits on which joints and game were roasted. Simpler arrangements for a revolving spit were to be found in most homes, down to the simplest farmhouse, where the joint would be trussed on to the spit, which was then suspended over the fire, by hooks attached to the fire dogs. The fat was caught in a dripping pan and the spit was turned either by a simple mechanical device or by hand, a small boy sometimes being detailed for the job.

Pots and kettles hung from large iron hooks above the fireplace and frying pans and saucepans were set over the fire on trivets. Bread was baked in an oven built into the brickwork of the chimney. This was first heated with a bundle of hot faggots and when they were removed and the bread put in, the oven was closed with an iron door. Bacon was smoked and cured in a smoke chamber formed in the flue of the fire and built at the side of the chimney.

In country districts, where difficulties of transport made coal expensive and wood was still used for fuel, the fire seldom

The earliest form of kitchen range, with an oven at the side of an open fire. c 1780

went out, the ashes remaining in the hearth and being stirred each morning till they sprang to life again.

In London coal had been used as the main fuel for many years. About 1780 the first kitchen range was designed, with an oven built on the side of an open fire. This meant that one side of the food cooked more than the other, so shelves were devised which twisted on a pivot. Early in the nineteenth century a boiler for hot water was fitted to this design, on the other side of the fire, but it had to be filled by hand. The next step was to furnish the fire with a cover, which served as a hot plate for boiling and stewing.

Lighting

Candles were used for lighting throughout the eighteenth century and were an expensive item in households which used many branched candelabra. At Houghton Hall the candles were said to cost £15 a night, but only a handful of people lived on that scale. Poor country people used home-make rush-lights as they had for generations. They were considerably cheaper than candles but did not give such a bright light.

The opening years of the nineteenth century saw the first experiments in gas lighting. Early installations in private

Rush-light holders. These were used by country people throughout the 18th century and well into the 19th century

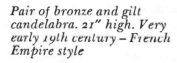

Pair of bronze and gilt candelabra. 21" high. Very early 19th century – French Empire style

Pair of silver candlesticks by Adam. 11" high

houses were formidably dangerous affairs and smelt abominably. The first experimental street lighting by gas was in 1810 but as late as 1828, when gas lighting had been installed at the Covent Garden Opera House, there was a serious explosion in the basement and the whole installation was scrapped, wax and oil lighting being put back for a while.

Oil lamps burning colza oil – a vegetable oil – were used during the 1830's but paraffin lamps did not come in till 1853.

Food and Drink

The basic diet of the English peasant was still bread, cheese and beer, with meat when times were good, fish when he could catch it and game when it came his way by poaching or any other method. For all but the unfortunates there was food in abundance and great variety.

Both rural and urban destitution existed and were going to increase, but the standards had a long way to drop yet, before they reached the depths of misery in which some of the labouring people were to exist during the middle years of the ninteenth century.

With the increasing supplies of fresh meat, made available by the practice of winter feeding, prodigious quantities were eaten, particularly of beef, but also of veal, mutton and lamb. Venison was for the landed gentry, who frequently distributed gifts of it to their friends and neighbours. Poultry was cheap and plentiful and so was fish, for the rivers were not yet polluted. Salmon was still being caught at the salmon-fishery at Putney and London fishermen could make a good living from the Thames. Large country households still had well-stocked fishponds for the coarser fish, such as carp, perch, tench and eels, and as transport improved supplies from Billingsgate and the coast reached ever farther inland.

Dairy products were plentiful and it was usual for quite small households to keep a cow and make their own butter and cheese. Indeed, as Jane Austen tells us, it was a mark of gentility for a family to keep its own cow.

Sugar, sometimes in large loaves weighing as much as twenty-two pounds, dried fruit and spices, including pepper, nutmeg and cinnamon, were imported regularly and were easily available at the grocers in most market towns.

Nearly all gardens had fruit trees and a vegetable patch, where potatoes, green vegetables, carrots, onions and turnips, cucumbers and salads were grown, and the diaries of these times are full of details of gifts of apples, nectarines, peaches, strawberries, apricots, filberts and walnuts made between

I *The Old East India Wharf at London Bridge*

A View in the Garden of Mr Aislabie Esqr at Studley in Yorkshire.

II   *A Landscaped Garden in Yorkshire*

III   *Covent Garden Market in the mid-eighteenth century,
from a painting by Samuel Scott*

IV *Blenheim Palace*

v   *A Coffee-House Scene, by Thomas Rowlandson*

VI *Adam Chimney-Piece,* 1772

VII *An Eighteenth-Century Shop Front: Fribourg and Treyer
in the Haymarket*

THE TIMES

OR DAILY UNIVERSAL REGISTER

NUMB. 940. TUESDAY, JANUARY 1, 1788. (Price Three-pence.)

VIII *The Front Page of the Times, January 1, 1788*

friends and neighbours, as well as trout, salmon, pigeons and game. Imported lemons and oranges were quite cheap but the more exotic fruits, particularly pineapples, were still very expensive.

Quantities of home-brewed ale, beer, porter, mead, cider, home-made wines and imported French, Spanish and Portuguese wines were drunk. Rum came from the West Indies. French brandy was expensive, for it carried a heavy import duty, but very large quantities were smuggled into the country. Gin was distilled from English corn and its manufacture was encouraged for a time. This, according to Defoe, was because it consumed such large quantities of corn that the farmers and large landowners reaped handsome profits. After the import duties were imposed on wine and brandy, gin was manufactured in England in such vast amounts that it was cheaper than beer, and during the 1730's and 40's there were said to be between six thousand and seven thousand gin shops in London alone. The poor drank so much of it that they died in their thousands. By 1751 the situation was so grave that gin was taxed and people were not allowed to sell it without a licence.

Tea, coffee and chocolate were all drunk, but only by the comparatively well-to-do, for they were expensive, tea, in particular, being very heavily taxed. However, during the later part of the eighteenth century more tea was smuggled into the country than arrived by the orthodox routes, and it was during these years that the poor, no longer able to afford the heavily taxed gin, managed to get hold of supplies of illicit tea and learnt to like it.

Meals

Breakfast was a simple meal. Labourers on rising had a mug of beer or tea and some bread. During the earliest part of the century, when times were better for them than they were later, they usually had meat or cheese as well. They took similar food with them for their midday meal and had their main

65

meal of the day when work finished in the early evening.

For the rest of the population breakfast was equally light, tea and bread and butter for most, or the more elegant coffee or chocolate. Early in the century a middle-day dinner was the principal meal of the day. As the century wore on the time of dinner moved to two or three o'clock, followed by tea-drinking in the late afternoon and a substantial supper about nine. As the dinner hour advanced people took to having a light snack in the middle of the morning. With the nineteenth century, the fashionable dinner hour grew later still, till it was in the early evening, after tea, and the mid-morning snack became a luncheon, taken about one o'clock.

Table Appointments

Georgian silver, glass and china were as beautiful in design and workmanship as the furniture, but amongst the lower middle classes the old pewter platters and mugs could still be found and country folk were still using their wooden trenchers until well into the nineteenth century.

1. Pewter tankards
2. Wooden and pewter trenchers
3. Wooden measure
   These were used by country people throughout the 18th century until china and glass were available to them

4. Silver coffee pot – 1765
5. Silver salver – 1733
6. Staffordshire tea-pot – c. 1750
7. Jacobite wine glasses – c. 1750

66

Chapter Five

SCIENCE AND MEDICINE

During the eighteenth century, many of the theories and scientific laws established by Newton and other distinguished scientists of Stuart days were developed and applied to practical inventions. These new devices, some made by practising craftsmen, others by theoretical experimenters, were, in the course of the century, to bring about fundamental changes in the lives of many English people. From country dwellers they became industrial and factory workers. The change is called the Industrial Revolution, but it came very slowly at first, gathering rapid momentum during the nineteenth century. Ultimately it brought many benefits, but in the course of the change many people suffered terrible hardships, for in the end industry expanded far too quickly, and a sense of responsibility on the part of the government and the wealthy developed far too slowly, for the necessary social changes to keep pace.

PURE SCIENCE
Chemistry
During Stuart times Robert Boyle had examined the relationship between the volume and pressure of air. Now Joseph Black of Glasgow succeeded in isolating one of the gases of the atmosphere, which later became known as carbon dioxide. Joseph Priestley, the Unitarian minister, who lived from 1733 to 1804, made many experiments in chemistry and electricity and discovered the existence of oxygen. Shortly afterwards, Henry Cavendish (1731–1810) was preparing 'inflammable

gas' or hydrogen, by dissolving zinc in acid, and from it, with the help of his friend James Watt, was able to deduce the chemical composition of both air and water.

The number of these scientists was very small and they compared their results with chemists and physicists all over Europe who were working on similar lines.

The Swedish apothecary, Scheele, isolated many chemical compounds for the first time during these years and it was Lavoisier, the French chemist in charge of the making of gunpowder in the laboratory of the Paris arsenal, who finally made clear the chemical processes involved when a substance is burned.

Lavoisier brought order into the science of chemistry. He was the first to use the word 'element' and gave the compounds names which indicated their composition. He was born in 1743, but his life was cut short in 1794, when he was sent to the guillotine by the French revolutionaries, who said the Republic had no need of learned men.

John Dalton, the north country schoolmaster, born in 1766, published *A New System of Chemical Philosophy* in 1808, in which he declared that every substance was made up of an enormous number of atoms and that these atoms were indestructible. He also suggested that the atoms of different substances had different weights, that chemical combinations consisted of the union of atoms, the same compounds always containing the same proportion of elements, and that when two elements combined to give several different compounds,

Humphry Davy's safety lamp for miners

the various amounts of each element will bear a simple numerical relationship to each other.

The Swedish chemist Berzelius developed Dalton's work, devising the chemical symbols which are in use today, and the Italian, Avogadro, prepared the way for the establishment of approximate atomic weights.

Magnetism and Electricity

In May, 1746, the Duchess of Bedford, in a letter to the Duke, who was visiting Bath for treatment for his gout, wrote: 'I supped at the Duchess of Montagu's on Tuesday night, where was Mr. Baker of the Royal Society, who electrified; it really is the most extraordinary thing one can imagine.'

Phenomena associated with static electricity had been known and observed for some time and Priestley devised a machine for producing electricity by friction, but there was no knowledge of an electric current until Galvani and Volta, two eighteenth century Italian professors, produced one in a battery composed of zinc and copper plates.

The news of this experiment reached the Royal Society in London and English scientists were soon making their own experimental batteries. Humphry Davy, born in 1778, managed to produce a 'column of electric light' from a battery. He also invented the miners' safety lamp and in the course of chemical experiments noticed that nitrous oxide gas made people insensible. This was the gas which later was given to dental patients.

Many experiments in electricity were now made. Humphry Davy became director of the Royal Institution in Albemarle Street and it was fashionable to attend his lectures and demonstrations, though few could have yet visualised their future practical applications.

One member of his audience was a book binder's apprentice, Michael Faraday. He was fascinated and ultimately became Davy's assistant and then began researches on his own acount, following up the new European discoveries of electro-

magnetism. Faraday, born in 1791, lived on into the later part
of the nineteenth century, and his achievement was the first
magneto-electric machine or 'dynamo'. Faraday's 'dynamo' in
time enabled electricity to be produced on a large scale and
led to the invention of the telephone, the telegraph and other
electrical devices of the Victorian era.

Gas

Gas lighting was first demonstrated in England very early in
the nineteenth century but the first gas cooker was not shown
to the world till the Great Exhibition of 1851.

Industrial Machinery

The few machines which intelligent craftsmen had devised
up till the beginning of Georgian times, as for example, saw
mills, stocking frames and looms, were made of wood, connected by metal joints. With a knowledge of chemistry,
machine makers were able to develop methods of using metal,
particularly iron, for making machines which were much
stronger and more effective.

Iron, the most widely spread of all metals, does not occur
freely in nature, but combined with other elements, usually
oxygen, in the form of oxides. Mankind has been smelting iron
for centuries and up till the sixteenth century the method was
to burn layers of ore and charcoal in a furnace, raised to a
fierce heat by bellows, until the charcoal combined with the
oxygen in the ore, leaving iron, which contained both carbon
and a compound of iron and carbon. Iron thus produced can
be melted and cast into moulds and is known as cast iron.
Another form of iron, obtained by oxidising the carbon from
the iron, can be hammered and shaped when it is molten and
is known as wrought iron.

Steel is another form of iron. For centuries this was made
by heating wrought iron with charcoal and then plunging the
red-hot mass in water. It produced a metal of great strength
and hardness which could be ground to produce a keen cutting

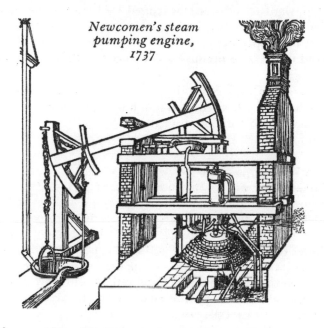

Newcomen's steam pumping engine, 1737

edge for swords and knives.

By the middle of the eighteenth century, coke, which is the residue from coal after certain elements have been distilled from it, was in general use for iron smelting. As iron deposits in this country occur near the coalfields where the coke was produced, the iron industry developed very quickly.

The Steam Engine

The use of steam as a source of power, to help that supplied by men and horses, had been discussed ever since Boyle had established his law that the volume of a given quantity of air, at constant temperature, varied in proportion to the pressure.

The first steam engine was invented by an ironmonger, Thomas Newcomen. It was a simple pumping engine, for pumping water out of coal mines, consisting of a boiler attached to a piston which moved up and down a cylinder.

The upward movement was caused by letting steam into the cylinder, the resultant high pressure causing it to rise. Then the steam supply was cut off and the cylinder cooled by a spray of cold water. The pressure was reduced and the piston moved down again.

At first the taps controlling the supply of steam and cold water had to be opened by hand, but an ingenious boy, growing bored with this job, invented valves which did the work for him.

James Watt (1736–1819)

James Watt was an instrument maker to the University of Glasgow. He examined Newcomen's engine and devised a new model which dispensed with the wasteful process of alternately heating and cooling the cylinder. He separated the cylinder from the condenser and kept it permanently hot with a steam jacket. Watt's steam engine used only a quarter of the fuel of Newcomen's and was employed not only to pump water from the steadily deepening coal mines but also for blowing the blast of air necessary to iron smelting.

In 1777 Watt, writing of a new pumping engine he had just installed, said 'the velocity, violence, magnitude and horrible noise of the engine gave universal satisfaction.'

Later he was to develop a machine which gave not only an up and down motion but also a rotary motion.

Steamboats

The next step was to try and fit a steam engine into a boat and make it drive paddle wheels. The first steam engines, including Newcomen's 'fire-engine', were so heavy that they almost sank the boats and the experiments were regarded as highly dangerous and impractical. However, an American artist who emigrated to Britain as a young man, Robert Fulton, managed to design a seaworthy steamboat and by 1825 the General Steam Navigation Company of Britain had fifteen small steamers trading between London and Europe.

An early cross-channel steamboat

Steam Locomotives

Experiments were also being made in steam locomotives. George Stephenson (1781–1848) was a child of the new industrial slums of the late eighteenth century and his first job was to help his father shovel coal into the furnace of one of Watt's pumping engines. He developed a passion for engines and when he was seventeen taught himself to read in order to find out more about them. He began to experiment and eventually his employers agreed to his supervising the construction of a steam locomotive.

His first engine achieved four miles an hour and consumed so much coal that the old horse-drawn trucks proved both cheaper and quicker. Undeterred, Stephenson made modifications and produced a model which burnt less fuel and had more power, and this was adopted in many mining districts for transporting coal and other heavy goods.

In 1825 the first goods railway was opened, to make the short run between Stockton and Darlington. The maximum speed was sixteen miles an hour and during the first year these locomotives were condemned as being too expensive, unreliable in a high wind, a danger to grazing cattle and against all the laws of Providence. But Stephenson foretold that before long they would be used for passengers and many agreed with him, prepared the ground and began to lay tracks. A prize was

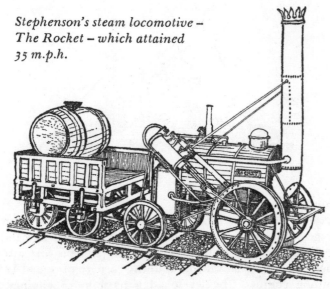

*Stephenson's steam locomotive –
The Rocket – which attained
35 m.p.h.*

offered for a new design and Stephenson won it with his Rocket, which attained thirty-five miles an hour. In 1830 it was used to inaugurate a passenger service between Liverpool and Manchester. Then Liverpool was joined by rail to Birmingham. Quickly a network of railways spread over the North of England, used mainly for the transport of coal and heavy industrial equipment but also for a few intrepid passengers.

Mrs. Fitzherbert, writing to her adopted daughter in 1835, said: 'I had set my mind upon going to see the famous railway at Liverpool, which is only about seven miles from this place . . .' but by the time she died, two years later, the railways were spreading down to London and the south and the novelty was over.

Submarines

Fulton had been in France during the Napoleonic wars, where he designed a submarine for the French government.

His 'Nautilus', with a three man crew, had a watertight hull, some twenty feet long by six feet wide, with a rounded, glass-sided conning tower. The keel was a large tank of water ballast and the weapon a looped, metal spike sticking out of the conning tower, which could be driven under the keel of an enemy ship. A rope attached to the spike was towed away and then a barrel of gunpowder hauled back to the keel and fired.

The French government was greatly impressed with this device but finally rejected it as being too barbarous a weapon even for warfare.

Balloons

Though Leonardo da Vinci had made experiments with flying machines and balloons during the fifteenth and early sixteenth centuries, it was not till the end of the eighteenth century that the Frenchman Montgolfier, with the help of his brother, invented the first practical balloon. It was a spherical bag of silk-covered paper, about thirty feet in diameter. Below it was attached a basket for the passengers and also for a fire made of straw and rags and about 400 lbs. of ballast. When the fire was lit, the hot air inflated the bag. The mooring ropes were detached and the balloon, belching forth smoke and flames from the fire basket, soared into the air, the passengers controlling the height of the balloon by regulating the fuel supply and throwing out ballast. A little later, hydrogen-filled balloons dispensed with the alarmingly dangerous fire baskets and watching balloon ascents became an amusement both in France and England.

In his diary for 1785 Parson Woodforde describes the misadventure of Major Money, whose balloon came down in the sea, where he remained '5 hours up to his chin . . . before he was taken up, and then by chance.'

The following year Sophie v. La Roche, staying in Dover, described the successful flight of Blanchard and Jeffries from Dover to Calais in three hours. Sophie remarked that 'this incident seemed to be remarkable in that so few people of

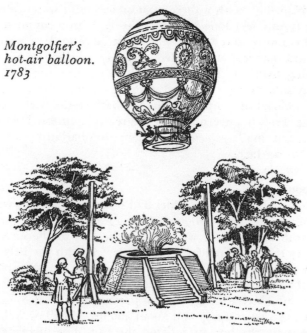

Montgolfier's hot-air balloon. 1783

standing or particular intellect were present, only the populace came to see.'

The undaunted Major Money strongly advocated the use of balloons in war. The French used captive balloons during the Napoleonic wars, but there was no great further development in their use till the end of the nineteenth century.

Spinning and Weaving Machines

In the early years of the Georgian period spinners and weavers worked mainly in their own homes and nearly half of England's export trade was of woollen cloth woven from English wool. Among her imports was an increasing amount of raw American cotton, which arrived at Liverpool and was spun and woven in the surrounding Lancashire towns and villages, where the damp climate proved highly suitable for its handling.

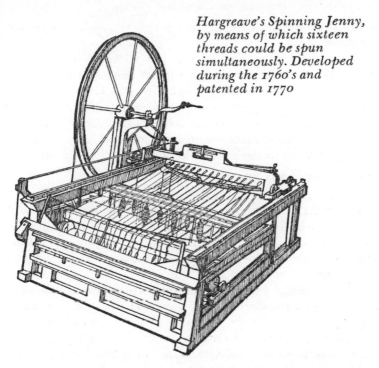

Hargreave's Spinning Jenny, by means of which sixteen threads could be spun simultaneously. Developed during the 1760's and patented in 1770

The spinning wheel had supplanted the hand-spindle by the sixteenth century, but spinning was still a slow process, and it took ten spinners to keep a weaver at work. Many experiments were made in an attempt to speed up the spinning process. Richard Arkwright of Bolton devised a machine driven by water power, and in 1764 William Hargreaves invented the Spinning Jenny, by which sixteen or more threads could be spun simultaneously by one spinner. It was a great step forward, but was more suitable for the spinning of wool than the fine cotton threads.

In 1774, however, Samuel Crompton, also of Bolton, invented his 'mule', which produced an excellently fine thread. The mule produced a yarn faster than the weaver could use it, but within a few years a fly shuttle had been invented which doubled the weaver's output, and in 1785 Cartwright perfected the power loom.

Water power was used at first, but within a few years of James Watt's invention, steam engines were installed in the cotton and woollen mills of Yorkshire and Lancashire. The days of the cottage spinners and weavers were now numbered. Steam driven machinery meant more factories, and cottagers, finding their hand-made home industries no longer needed, tended to move to the towns where they were being built.

MEDICINE AND SURGERY
Medicine

The Royal College of Physicians was already a powerful body by the beginning of the eighteenth century, but only men who had studied at Oxford, Cambridge or Trinity College, Dublin, were admitted to full membership. These Fellows were a small but august body who charged high fees and received handsome incomes from their treatment of the rich. Licentiates of the College were members who had studied at Edinburgh or one of the European medical schools, of which Leyden had the highest prestige at this time. They, too, had flourishing practices, mainly in London or the larger provincial cities.

Not only were there too few of these doctors, but their charges were too high for most people, who mainly sought advice from the apothecaries. The apothecaries had originally been members of the Grocers' Company, and as tradesmen had dispensed medicines from doctors' prescriptions. In time, to the annoyance of the College of Physicians, they began to prescribe medicines on their own account, and by the middle of the eighteenth century they were recognized as general medical practitioners. They would call on a qualified physician to advise in a difficult case. At first they were not allowed to charge consultation fees, so they put up the price of their medicines, but by 1815 a full member of the Society of Apothecaries was entitled to charge a professional fee for a consultation.

Surgeons

Surgeons still belonged to the Company of Barbers but in 1745 they broke away and founded their own Company of Surgeons. With no available anaesthetics, the scope of the operations they could perform was very limited, but with the patient strapped firmly to the operating table and often made partly insensible with alcohol, the surgeons achieved extraordinary speed and dexterity in such matters as amputating a limb or trephining a skull. As early as 1694 a successful operation for cataract was performed on Lady Rachel Russell and in 1767 her grandson, the fourth Duke of Bedford, was similarly treated.

During the reigns of Queen Anne and George I the two great London hospitals were St. Bartholemew's and St. Thomas's. St. Thomas's was rebuilt about this time and many improvements made at St. Bartholomews, both in the teaching and the treatment and housing of the patients. By 1745, the year of the last Jacobite rebellion, Guy's, the Westminster, St. George's, the London and Middlesex hospitals had all been founded by individual philanthropists and many others were established in county towns throughout the country.

These hospitals were free, but in order to gain admittance patients usually had to have some pull in the form of a special recommendation from one of the governors. At Barts you had to put down a burial fee of 19/6d, but it was handed back to you if you recovered.

The greatest surgeon and teacher of the eighteenth century was John Hunter (1728–1793). He impressed on his students the importance of a knowledge of physiology as well as anatomy in surgery. At his home in Kensington he carried out hundreds of experiments and observations on animals, birds, fishes and insects; and in the field of comparative anatomy he did work far in advance of his contemporaries.

The schools of surgery in the teaching hospitals were doing increasingly useful work as the century drew to a close and in 1800 the Royal College of Surgeons was founded, surgeons being given a professional status equal to that of the physicians.

Medicine and Public Health

The doctors still could not take a pulse accurately, for watches with second hands were not yet made. They had no thermometers, no antiseptics and no anaesthetics, for the first operation under ether anaesthesia was not performed in Britain until 1846. Nevertheless, one of the reasons for the rapid increase in population during the eighteenth century was undoubtedly the advance in medical treatment and the beginning of preventive medicine, which greatly reduced the death rate, particularly amongst children and mothers in childbirth.

Sir John Pringle (1702–1782), an army physician, saw that gaol fever or typhus was the same as hospital fever. Most people regarded this disease as an unavoidable scourge, but Sir John noticed that it occurred where people were in contact with decomposing matter. He ensured that in the hospitals under his charge the drainage was adequate and the water supply as pure as possible. He even suggested the use of substances which in the nineteenth century were to be called antiseptics.

As the necessity for pure water was more fully appreciated towns demanded better water supplies, but they were a very long time coming and there were terrible cholera epidemics in England as late as the first half of the last century. However, deep wells and springs were now used in preference to surface water and streets were cleaned, widened and paved. Ancient open drains were covered, the pestilential Fleet Ditch in the City of London being almost completely filled in by the 1760's.

Though surgeons extended the field of their operations and gained considerable success in the initial stages, the death rate of surgical patients in the hospitals was about two in three, mainly because the necessity for antiseptic precautions was not appreciated. The operating theatres were lit by candles

The Fleet Ditch in the City of London, which was filled in during the 18th century

or lamps, they had no running water and the floors were sprinkled with sawdust to cover the bloodstains. The surgeon wore a special 'dirty' coat for his work. Instruments received only a perfunctory cleaning and probes, scissors and sponges passed from patient to patient and from wound to wound. Midwives, too, would go from case to case, and through ignorance of the first principles of sterilising themselves and their instruments, spread puerperal fever and death.

Sir James Young Simpson, the famous Scottish surgeon who was to discover the uses of chloroform, said that 'a patient on the operating table was exposed to greater danger than the soldier on the field of Waterloo.'

Smallpox

There was no recurrence of the seventeenth century plague during the eighteenth century. One reason for this was probably that houses were now built of brick or stone instead of wood, through which the flea-carrying plague rat could not gnaw its way.

In place of the plague, smallpox was the eighteenth century

scourge and at one time it was killing a tenth of the population each year. As early as 1717 Lady Mary Wortley Montague had written to London about a process of inoculation against smallpox which she had seen practised in Turkey, and an inoculation hospital was opened in London, which had a certain measure of success, people being inoculated with what Lady Mary described as 'the matter of the best sort of smallpox', but it was found that sometimes people inoculated in this way infected those who had not been inoculated.

So dreaded was the disease that parsons would sometimes refuse to bury victims, and when Mr. Cole of Bletchley was burying one of his parishioners, her son-in-law refused to wear the special black mourning cloak supplied by the undertakers, for fear of being infected, and borrowed Mr. Cole's Master of Arts gown instead.

It was Jenner (1740–1823), a pupil of the great John Hunter, who observed that after a mild dose of smallpox people became immune to the disease and that cowmen after handling cattle with cowpox did not develop it at all. He began inoculating with cowpox and by the end of the century the use of this vaccine had controlled the disease.

The Window Tax

Lack of fresh air and much ill-health was caused by the hated window tax. It had first appeared in 1696 when houses with less than ten windows paid 2/- a year and houses with ten to twenty windows paid 2/- and an additional 4/- a year and was steadily increased, particularly during the Seven Years War and the Napoleonic wars. For people with fair-sized houses and a number of windows it became a serious burden. The result was that many people blocked up some of their windows, sometimes too many for health and comfort. The window tax was not repealed till 1851, by which time the Exchequer was receiving well over £1,700,000 a year from it, and old houses with blocked windows can still be seen in many parts of the country.

False teeth presented a problem, for no one had yet thought of an effective way of taking an impression of the mouth. Mrs. Purefroy sent to Mr. Coryndon, 'Operator for ye Teeth near the new Church in ye Strand,' for a set of teeth, marking on a piece of wood the places where her own teeth remained and giving the measurement of her gums on a piece of tape. But when the set arrived she complained that the spaces he had left did not correspond with her own teeth and the bite was too high on the two 'hind' teeth.

Henry had a good collection of spectacles – horn, tortoise-shell and silver-rimmed – which were sent to London from time to time to be repaired, but the lenses, which were Concave Number Six, he bought separately and preferred to put in himself.

Bloodletting was still practised, oddly enough for such complaints as tuberculosis, and when, in 1767, the young Marquis of Tavistock fractured his skull in a hunting accident, he was trephined two or three times before he died.

Tunbridge Wells was no longer as fashionable as it had been when Queen Mary had gone there to take the waters, but Cheltenham and Bath were both fashionable in the second half of the eighteenth century and there were many other smaller spas which have since been forgotten.

Dr. Jenner inoculating a child against smallpox. Late 18th century

Chapter Six

AGRICULTURE AND INDUSTRY

Agriculture

In early Georgian times more than three quarters of the population were still country dwellers and large tracts of the English countryside were still cultivated on the medieval, open field system. This was a survival of the time when the feudal lord of the manor, while retaining a proportion of land for his own use, allowed the rest to be cultivated by the peasants living on the manor for their own use. In return, they worked for two or three days a week on the lord's land. Fields were not enclosed by hedges. They often extended for several miles and were divided into strips of approximately 22 yards by 220 yards long, each peasant being allotted one or more strips in each field. They were cultivated in a three-year rotation, the first year being planted with wheat, the second with barley or oats and the third year they lay fallow.

At the beginning of the eighteenth century there were still some two million agricultural labourers who derived some of their subsistence from a free stake in the land, even if it were only the right to graze a cow or a few pigs on the village common land – and that number represented nearly a half of the entire population.

As the population of the country increased and food production on a larger scale became necessary, the disadvantages of the open field method of cultivation became increasingly apparent. The first important enclosures of land had taken place in Tudor times and had caused great concern and outbreaks of rioting amongst the dispossessed peasants, though most people agreed that in the long run enclosure made for better farming.

By the 1700's most of the south eastern counties had been enclosed, including the orchards and hop fields of Kent. The important agricultural regions of the west country were also enclosed, but the valuable wheatlands of the midlands and parts of East Anglia were still open fields.

Jethro Tull

Early in the eighteenth century, a Berkshire gentleman farmer, Jethro Tull, began to examine the actual growth of plants and discovered the principle by which their cultivation should be regulated. Instead of the ancient method of broadcasting the seed at sowing time, he made experiments in sowing seeds in straight drills, with the rows wide enough apart for the ground to be properly hoed and broken up round the plants, so that the roots could receive full nourishment from the soil. He found that with this new, orderly method of sowing and cultivation the yield from his seeds was increased nearly five-fold.

He invented a new type of plough, which broke up the land more effectively, and a mechanical drill, which made the channels for the seed, released it from a seed box, and covered it with earth, all in one process.

Jethro Tull's seed-drill 1733

In 1731 he published his results in a work entitled *Horse-Hoeing Husbandry or An Essay on the Principle of Tillage and Vegetation*. The small farmers of England, with little capital for making experiments even if they had wanted to, continued farming in the same old way, most of them never having heard about the book, but large landowners, in particular Lord Townshend of Raynham Hall in Norfolk, became interested in Tull's new methods, his explanations of the true use of manure and his insistence on the necessity for pulverising the soil during cultivation.

Small quantities of turnips had been grown in English vegetable gardens for a long time and their usefulness as winter cattle food had been suggested from time to time, but up till now conservative English farmers had never tried out the idea of growing turnips in large quantities in order to keep their cattle alive during the winter and continued the wasteful practice of killing off most of them in the late autumn. Lord Townshend, however, was a turnip enthusiast, and with Tull's improved methods of cultivation began growing turnips on a large scale as winter cattle fodder – hence his nickname of Turnip Townshend.

Turnip Townshend

In place of the old three-year rotation in open fields Lord Townshend introduced the four-course Norfolk system in enclosed fields, with wheat the first year, oats or barley the second, clover, rye, vetches, swedes and kale the third and turnips for the fourth year. In this way he was able to feed more sheep and cattle during the winter and also obtain more manure for his land: and by avoiding the fallow year he saved one third of his land from being wasted each year.

Robert Bakewell

About the same time as these Norfolk experiments, Robert Bakewell, of Leicestershire, was experimenting in the breeding of English oxen and sheep, which hitherto had been leggy

Leicestershire long-horn bull

beasts, with meat of a not particularly high quality. Sheep in particular had been valued more for their wool than their meat, but now the quality was greatly improved and Bakewell's Leicestershire breed of sheep became famous. For some years his hardy Leicestershire longhorn cattle were almost as popular, but when, later in the century, the shorthorn breed was evolved by two Durham brothers, shorthorns became increasingly popular and the herds of longhorns dwindled.

Bakewell also bred a new and improved type of farm horse. He was an excellent farmer and devised a system of irrigation for improving his grasslands.

The later and more popular short-horn breed

Arthur Young

Arthur Young, a farmer who became secretary of the Board of Agriculture, advocated strongly the work of these three pioneers, and his enthusiasm now inspired farmers to try these new experiments for themselves, but how was it to be done with the old open field system to which they were tied? When the corn was harvested from the various strips, in the late summer, the whole field was made available for everyone's cattle to pasture. If an enterprising farmer planted his own strip with turnips, in order to feed his own cattle during the winter, there were no fences or hedges to stop someone else's cattle wandering all over the crop and eating it. The answer was more enclosures. The big landlords began the process, offering compensation, which was usually fixed by act of Parliament, to those who were dispossessed.

The new system spread rapidly and before long the rolling open fields of the midlands were transformed to a patchwork of small enclosures with neat, new hedges.

The overall result was a great increase in the production of corn, both for beer and bread, as well as supplies of fresh meat during the winter, instead of the salted meat which had been responsible for so much suffering from scurvy. But the immediate result, from the villagers' point of view, was good times for the landowners, who were now enjoying a greatly increased rent-roll, and hard times for themselves. Those who did not become labourers on the newly-organized farms existed for a while on cottage industries and then, with the development of steam-driven machinery and the building of factories to house it, they drifted to the new industrial towns to seek a living.

Small, independent farmers suffered too, particularly if they lacked capital for the new equipment and farming machinery, or even the money for fencing, which was a considerable item. They soon found themselves unable to compete with the more advanced methods of farming and many voluntarily sold out to the bigger men.

Thomas Coke

During the later half of the eighteenth century another Norfolk farmer, Thomas Coke of Holkham, Earl of Leicester, was one of the first to use oil cake and bone manure. He established the different feeding values of various grasses and advocated long leases to tenant farmers, as an incentive to good farming.

George III – Farmer George – was keenly interested in all these farming experiments and when Arthur Young was publishing his *Annals of Farming* the King, under the name of Mr Ralph Robinson, supplied him with information from his own experimental farm at Petersham.

The Corn Laws

The increase in the country's food supply was timely, for there was a ready-made market for it in the rapidly growing industrial areas. By the end of the century we had already begun to import wheat, but these supplies were cut off by the French blockade, during the Napoleonic wars. The demand for home-grown wheat increased and if it had not been available we should have starved.

The price of English wheat soared. In 1793 it was 50/- a quarter and by 1812 it had risen to 126/- a quarter. The farmers prospered and the labourers and factory workers, whose wages were not pegged to the rising cost of living, suffered grieviously. With the end of the war and renewed imports from Europe, as well as America and Canada, the price dropped again for a while and the farmers howled with anguish, complaining that they faced ruin. The Corn Laws were passed, to keep the price of wheat at a level which gave the farmers a fair profit, but they made life more difficult than ever for the underpaid workers, for whom bread was the principal item of food, as for the vast army of unemployed soldiers who returned to England after the wars.

Industry

At the beginning of the eighteenth century the export of English woollen cloth represented nearly half the value of our foreign trade and, next to agriculture, spinning and weaving were our most important industries. They were still rural, cottage industries, and as the enclosing of land increased and so many country folk lost their right to farm the village lands, spinning and weaving became increasingly important sources of income for them, for this was still a hand-made world.

Itinerant chapmen trudged through the countryside with huge packs of raw materials to sell and large bales of finished yarn and cloth which they had bought from customers and were prepared to sell to any who wanted it. Sometimes they travelled on foot, with their packs humped on their backs, sometimes they could afford a pack horse.

The larger farming households bought yarn from the chapman as well as the cottager, for many farms, particularly in Yorkshire and Lancashire, had a long tradition of spinning and weaving, with two or three looms installed in their outhouses. The womenfolk – housewife, daughters, servants and dairy maids – did the spinning in their spare time and the menfolk the weaving.

Apprenticeship was still the rule for entry into the weaving industry, for apprenticeship was the old English school of craftsmanship, but it was beginning to break down. People were setting up as weavers, and indeed in other industries, without having served their time, and it was difficult to check them, while amongst the spinners children were set to work in their own homes when they were only three or four years old, years before they were even old enough to be apprenticed to a master.

This was the wool industry till the mechanical inventions of the later part of the century resulted in steam-driven machinery for spinning and weaving and the ultimate establishment of the woollen factories in central Yorkshire, mainly in the towns of Bradford and Leeds, midway between the coal

In the early 18th century spinning was one of Britain's most important industries. There were no factories, so people did the work at home, in their cottages. Little girls were taught to spin by their mothers when they were still very young

mines of south Yorkshire and the wool supplies of the northern part of the country. By this time supplies of wool were already being imported but it was not till the end of the nineteenth century that supplies began to arrive from Australia and New Zealand.

Spitalfield Silk Weavers

A group of weavers who steadfastly refused to use power looms were the Huguenot silk weavers who had settled in the fields outside Bishopsgate at the end of the seventeenth century. Spitalfields silk weaving became a flourishing industry and the population of the district rapidly increased. By 1832 there were 50,000 people in Spitalfields dependent on the silk weaving industry and some 15,000 looms at work, in their attractive little Georgian terraced cottages, weaving thousands of yards of expensive velvet and silk, much of which was exported, but with the competition of power looms they fell on hard times and the few weaving families who survived into the present century, the last to practice the art of hand silk weaving, were desperately poor and ill-paid, ekeing out a living by making silk cloth for expensive neckties and Jewish praying shawls.

Lace

Lace-making was a valuable cottage industry, for quantities of lace were worn, particularly during the earlier part of the century. The business flourished around Honiton and also in Bedfordshire and Buckinghamshire. There was an important lace market at Newport Pagnell and Mr Cole of Bletchley was a great friend of James and Nathaniel Cartwright, the lace merchants who divided their time between their home in London and their lace-makers in Buckinghamshire. They were a convivial pair and Mr Cole described how Nathaniel, on his way back from the Newport lace market, hurt his ankle, for 'I suppose he got drunk'. However, a week or two later, though still lame, Nathaniel set off 'on his long journey into the North and by Gloucester, with above £1,000 of lace.'

Cotton

The cotton industry also began as a cottage industry. Cotton or 'cotton wool' as it was called for a long time, had been imported in small quantities from the Near East for many years, to make wicks for candles. The Levant Company took over this trade for candle wicks at the beginning of the seventeenth century, but no one in England thought of using it for textiles yet, though the East India Company began the import of a variety of cotton fabrics from India.

Weavers invariably used up yarn more quickly than the spinners could produce it and on one occasion, when there was a shortage of linen yarn, some Lancashire weavers experimented with 'cotton wool' from the Levant as a weft thread combined with linen as a warp. This new material was highly successful but the cotton wool could only be supplied by the London importers after they had met the requirements of the candle-makers.

Lace-making was a valuable cottage industry. Pillow lace was made like this well into the 20th century, particularly in Bedfordshire and Buckinghamshire

With the development of the West Indian and American colonies, the cotton plant was found growing wild and a few bags of cotton were sometimes included in the regular cargoes of sugar, rum and tobacco which now came to Bristol and London.

The popularity of cotton grew and merchants from Manchester and south Lancashire would make the long journey to London or Bristol in order to buy cotton, which they took back to their warehouses and distributed to the spinners as it was needed, thereby maintaining them with a steady supply.

The damp climate of Lancashire was particularly suitable for the handling of cotton, and before long imports were all arriving at Liverpool. In 1770 there were only two stage coaches a week between Liverpool and Manchester, but the scene was to change very quickly. In 1776 Brindley joined Manchester to Liverpool with the cutting of the Manchester Ship canal. The problem of carriage was eased and by the end of the century there were seventy coaches a week running between Liverpool and Manchester for the transport of the business men. As with the wool workers, the establishment of the power-driven mills

Luddites smashing weaving machines, because they feared they would take away their livelihoods of hand-weaving. 1811

at last brought the cottage cotton spinners and weavers into the towns. By the early nineteenth century America had become the chief cotton producing country in the world and Liverpool the largest importer of raw cotton.

In 1760 the cotton industry was using 8,000 tons of raw cotton, in 1800 25,000 tons and by 1830 100,000 tons.

The Luddites

Though some hand-workers accepted the change from the independence of their own homes to the routine of a factory and their dependence on the owners, many bitterly resisted the new order of things. They hated the machines and tried to destroy them. They sent threatening letters to the employers, signed King Lud, which gave them the name of the Luddites.

In 1811 they were smashing machines and burning factories in the North and the Midlands and the following year Lancashire hand-loom weavers burnt the factory at West Houghton and made attempts on many others, for which four of their number were hanged and seventeen were sentenced to transportation for seven years.

In Yorkshire wool workers smashed a machine which trimmed the nap of woollen cloth and was said to do the work of four men. Soldiers were called in to protect the woollen mills and fourteen Luddites were hanged.

The stocking knitters of Nottingham, Leicester and Derbyshire worked in their own homes, on machines supplied by the wholesale merchants, and throughout 1811 they smashed a thousand or more of these stocking frames as a protest against reduced wages during a trade depression.

These disturbances stopped only when the government, despite many protests from all walks of life, changed the penalty for frame-smashing from transportation to death by hanging. Wages remained low and the price of bread rose steadily.

Coal and Iron

In 1759 the Earl of Bridgwater had instructed his engineer, Brindley, to cut a canal between Manchester and the Duke's collieries at Worsley. A few years later the Manchester Ship canal was opened and many more canals were cut through the new industrial regions, which greatly eased the transport problem. Iron was necessary for the new machinery which developed from Hargreaves' Spinning Jenny of 1764, Watt's steam engine of 1765, Arkwright's spinning machine of 1768 and Crompton's mule of 1776, and for their manufacture large quantities of coal were needed for iron smelting. Coal was also the means of power to work these new inventions. Coal and iron became vitally important industries by means of which, during the Napoleonic wars, Britain was able to capture the cotton and wool trade and become the most important manufacturing country in the world.

Minerals, except gold and silver, were still considered the property of the landowners. Lord Dartmouth, for example, owned many of the Staffordshire mines. Several small mines

The head of a coal mine. Mid-18th century

existed which were worked by only two or three men and there was still a certain amount of surface mining, but generally speaking the mines were growing deeper and pit shafts as much as 400 feet were cut. There were many terrible accidents due to explosions from fire-damp, and flooding was a grave problem till the development of the pumping engine. Horses were used to pull the trucks of coal, on wooden rails, down to the river, and in the early days, before the canals and steam locomotives, twenty thousand horses were at work in the industry.

Coal production in 1770 was some 6,000,000 tons a year but by 1830 it had risen to 23,000,000 tons. Iron production was only about 250,000 tons in 1800 but by 1835 it had risen four-fold to 1,000,000 tons.

Other metals

The tin mines of Devon and Cornwall and the lead mines of Somerset and Derbyshire were all busy, as also were the Cornish copper mines. During the eighteenth century the main use of copper, apart from coins, was for pans and kettles, while lead was used for pipes and roofing and also for lead shot.

With the increasing use of china and porcelain from Staffordshire, pewter was going out of fashion. This meant that the demand for tin was declining, while as yet zinc was used only for mixing with copper to produce brass.

At the beginning of the nineteenth century Great Britain had the lead in the world metal trade, for most of the tin and copper in use in the world came from Cornwall and large quantities of lead were mined in the Pennines, the present great metal-producing regions of the world not having yet been developed.

The Potteries

Throughout the middle and later part of the eighteenth century there were many small English porcelain factories, producing work inspired by the porcelain and china brought back from the East by the East India Company. Amongst the most famous were those at Chelsea, Bow, Derby, Worcester and Lowestoft, all of which produced work which was very beautiful but also very expensive.

It was Josiah Wedgwood (1730–1795) who produced pottery and china which every one could afford and turned it out in

The Wedgwood potteries in the 1760's

D

such large quantities that it set the universal fashion for china-ware and the decline in the use of pewter.

Josiah Wedgwood inherited his family's small pottery business in Burslem, Staffordshire, which had manufactured an early English salt-glaze pottery. Round about 1725 the firm had been producing teapots with hard-fired red bodies covered with a coarse brown glaze, straight conical spouts and thick, loop handles. This was the first appearance of the old brown teapot, which was to supplant the even earlier tin or pewter pot.

Wedgwood perfected a white English earthenware and began to experiment. His shapes, colours and designs were excellent and he used John Flaxman, the sculptor, to design the characteristic Wedgwood decoration of classical figures, many of which were copied from the frescoes of Pompeii.

Wedgwood pottery was soon in demand abroad as well as at home and the transport of such delicate cargo was made possible by the steadily improving water communications of the later part of the eighteenth century, including the new Grand Junction canal, joining the Mersey to the Trent. This and other similar waterways made it possible for many goods, as well as coal for fuel, to be carried from the manufacturing towns of the midlands and the north not only to the ports but to the remoter parts of the country, which had up till this time been unable to obtain many goods which were now available.

All the time, the population was rapidly increasing and continued to absorb these new goods. It rose from about 8,000,000 in 1760 to 10,500,000 in 1801 and to 16,000,000 by 1831. It was during these years that Birmingham, Sheffield and Glasgow grew so rapidly, Birmingham specialising in small industries, Sheffield in cutlery and Glasgow in cotton.

Mechanisation in industry spread slowly, even in the textile industries. It has been estimated that by 1830, though practically all cotton spinning was done in steam factories, there were still 240,000 hand looms as compared with 60,000 power looms, though of course a power loom would turn out a far greater quantity of cotton cloth than a hand loom. There was even less mechanisation in the wool industry as yet and despite the early experiments in steam-ships, sailing ships were still supreme.

Ship-building was concentrated in the big ports but after the union of England and Scotland in 1707 Clydeside grew increasingly important as the home of British ship-building. In the years to come the industry was to develop in conjunction with metal engineering but this was still the day of wooden ships.

The Northampton boot and shoe industry was still mainly a hand industry although by 1830 a few factories with power-driven machinery had been established at Kettering: but such things as cutlery, carpets and furniture were all hand-made.

Chapter Seven

TRADE AND COMMERCE

The Slave Trade

With the development of the cotton trade of Liverpool came an appalling increase in the slave trade. At the Treaty of Utrecht, in 1713, Britain had won from France the monopoly of the slave trade to the Spanish American colonies and the Africa company undertook to deliver to them a minimum of 4,800 slaves a year, a quarter of the profits to go to the King of Spain and another quarter to Queen Anne. In addition to this, between 1680 and 1780, Britain imported well over 2,000,000 slaves to her own colonies in the West Indies and America.

London merchants had been first in the field with this slave trade, which was mostly from the Guinea coast and West Africa, but after the collapse of the South Sea Company, in 1720, which had attempted to capture the trade of Spanish America, many London merchants were ruined and lacked the capital to continue trading. The business fell into the hands of the Bristol men, already engaged in the import of American tobacco. They now travelled from Bristol to West Africa for cargoes of slaves, which they took across the Atlantic, returning home with their cargoes of tobacco. Liverpool merchants eyed their business enviously. Most of them lacked the capital to equip their own ships for similar trips, which might take anything up to twelve months, but they worked their way in by carrying Manchester goods across to the West Indies, where they sold them to Spanish smugglers who slipped them into the Spanish colonies free of the three hundred per cent duty im-

posed by the Spanish government. Spain protested in no un-
certain terms but it was another twenty years before the practice was stopped and in the meantime the Liverpool men had
made enormous profits and were able to compete and very soon
outpace the Bristol slavers. They loaded their ships with Manchester cottons specially made for the African trade, traded
them on the west coast of Africa for slaves, carried the slaves
across to America and returned with cargoes of raw cotton.

Little was known of the interior of Africa yet by Europeans
and all the trading was done on the coast. The African chiefs
or their agents supplied the slaves, many from amongst their
prisoners who had already been condemned to death: but if the
demand exceeded the supply they were not above making false
charges or promoting inter-tribal warfare in order to increase
their numbers of available prisoners.

Men, women and children were driven down to the coast,
sometimes a distance of two or three hundred miles, and
herded into the waiting slave ships, where conditions were
appalling. The men were chained in couples and crowded into
cabins which gave them about a square yard of living space,
and the accommodation for women and children was even
more cramped. During the periods when the slaves were
allowed on deck, a batch at a time, their fetters were fastened
to ring bolts in the deck, to stop them throwing themselves
overboard. The Atlantic crossing took seven or eight weeks.
Many did not survive and some, in such desperate misery,
deliberately starved themselves to death.

From the earliest days of the slave trade there had been
voices raised against it, particularly by the Quakers of Pennsyl-
vania and the Society for the Propagation of Christian Knowledge, which had been founded by the end of the seventeenth
century, but for many years their influence was not strong
enough and the slave trade was an extremely profitable business.

John Newton was the captain of a slave ship in his young
days. Later, after his ordination and appointment to Olney

*West African slaves being herded onto a slave ship bound for
America. Mid-18th century*

and then to St Mary, Woolnoth, his writing and preaching
against slavery gave valuable support to William Wilberforce's
campaign for the emancipation of the slaves. The Liverpool
slave trade was finally abolished in 1807, the year of Newton's
death, but he said that during the 1750's, when he was engaged
in the trade: 'I never had the least scruple as to its lawfulness.
I was upon the whole, satisfied with it, as the appointment
Providence had marked out for me . . . It is indeed accounted
a genteel employment . . . .'

The plea that such social evils were the will of a Divine providence was to bedevil the work of reformers for many years
to come.

During the later part of the century planters who had made
a fortune in the West Indian sugar-cane plantations occasionally brought slaves back to England as personal servants, and
for a while it was highly fashionable to have a Negro boy or
girl in attendance about the household. Sometimes they ran
away and advertisements and rewards for their recovery were
published in the newspapers. On occasion they were even put
up for sale. In 1769 the *Public Advertiser* was announce-
ing: 'To be sold, a Black Girl, 11 years of age; extremely handy;
works at her needle tolerably, and speaks English well. Inquire

of Mr Owen, at the "Angel" Inn, behind St Clement's Church, in the Strand.'

In 1772, as a result of protests from Granville Sharp, a test case was brought concerning one of these slaves, and the Lord Chief Justice decided that once a slave had set foot on British territory he was free and could not be taken back into slavery.

London

England was still mainly self-supporting in essentials during the eighteenth century, though she was already running short of timber for ship-building and house-building, which she was now importing from the American colonies and from the countries of the Baltic. Another vital necessity from the Baltic was tallow for tallow candles. However the high value of her exports of cotton and woollen cloth meant that she was able to import increasing quantities of luxuries. Though Liverpool was the port of entry for cotton and Bristol for tobacco, the Port of London was far larger and more important than any other. In any case the smoking of tobacco fell out of fashion during the later part of the eighteenth century and was considered rather vulgar. When in 1766 Archdeacon Gordon visited Newport Pagnell, and Mr Cole with forty-three other members of the clergy dined with him, Mr. Cole remarked in his diary: 'and what is extraordinary, not one smoaked Tobacco.' Parson Woodforde gave it up about this time and on more than one occasion recorded that he felt all the better for having done so.

Those who still clung to the habit smoked the long churchwarden pipes, but snuff was now the rage and an elegant snuff box was as essential an appurtenance to a man of fashion as was a fan to his lady.

The Russell family had a large interest in the East India Company. When, in 1696, Lord Tavistock married Elizabeth Howland, who brought to the Russells large areas of Streatham, Tooting Bec and Rotherhithe, his father, the first Duke, built a dry dock and then a wet dock at Rotherhithe.

The dry dock he leased to the Wells brothers and Wells' Yard was soon busy with ship-building. The wet dock, called the Howland dock, was used by the East India Company and the Russells had an interest in many of its ships, the Streatham, the Bedford, the Tavistock, the Russell and the Howland all being built at Wells' dock by the beginning of the eighteenth century.

The family would invest as much as £2,000 in a voyage and take a proportionate share of the profits. Sometimes they sent out their own bales of cloth, which had come up from the cloth merchants on their own estates at Tavistock and Exeter. Devon weavers sometimes dealt directly with the East India Company, but if they were short of capital and could not afford to wait for their money till the goods were sold, perhaps nine months or a year later, the Duke would either lend them the money or buy the goods speculatively himself and pay for them promptly.

Capital was vital for these long trading journeys and without the help of rich men they would not have been possible. The merchants of the City of London supplied the bulk of the finance for the East India Company, the Baltic, the Levant and the Hudson's Bay Fur Company. They took considerable risks for the voyages were fraught with many hazards. The wooden vessels could sink or catch fire. The Mediterranean was still infested by the Turkish corsairs, and pirates as desperate lurked off the coasts of Africa and roamed the Indian ocean, while during the French wars French privateers were always on the watch.

However, most of them got through and as the traffic increased the Pool of London grew busier every year. Traffic soon outstripped the port facilities, so that many ships had to ride at anchor in the fairway. The existing quays and wharves had to be enlarged, river walls maintained and the river bed required constant dredging. Warehouses had to be built to house the unloaded goods till such time as they could be marketed. Some are still standing, including those in Cutler Street, which were built between 1765 and 1782 by the old East India Dock Company.

Customs inspection was an increasing problem, for although the docks lay so close to the dignified City, which was growing in affluence and power each year, living on the river banks was the most disreputable collection of river pirates, night plunderers, mudlarks and receivers of all kinds.

Tea

The East India Company's tea agents were not allowed to land in China in the early days so they purchased their China and Japanese tea in Java: but in 1684 China allowed the Company to build a small trading station at Canton. Thereafter tea arrived in London in steadily increasing quantities. This was 'green' tea, in which the leaves were dried without fermentation, and it came to London in the company's slow and cumbersome windjammers, which were known as the tea wagons. A round trip took five or six months and until 1833 the East India Company held the monopoly of this trade.

About the turn of the century tea bushes were found growing wild in the jungles of Assam, in north-east India, but it was not till the early 1830's that the first Indian tea arrived in England. It was treated differently, the leaves being fermented during the drying process, to produce the black tea which is now more popular.

However, throughout the eighteenth century the popularity of green tea from China increased steadily, though it remained very expensive, for the government imposed an import duty of 5/- a pound. In the countries of Europe it was costing less than a shilling a pound and was an open invitation to smugglers. Business men supplied the capital and bought large quantities of tea in Europe, as well as brandy and tobacco, both of which were heavily taxed in England. The contraband was brought across the North Sea and the English Channel to previously agreed points, and under cover of darkness the English fishing boats would steal silently out to meet them, load their boats and return to shore, where willing hands were waiting to help them unload and store the precious cargo, in

Smugglers landing contraband cargoes of tea.
Mid-18th century

barns, sheds and cellars, to await further distribution either locally or amongst the merchants of London. The import tax was so resented that few had any compunction about breaking the law, even though the extreme penalty was hanging.

Adam Smith, the Scottish economist, described the smuggler as 'a person who, though no doubt highly blamable for violating the laws of his country, is frequently incapable of violating those of natural justice, and would have been in every respect an excellent citizen had not the laws of his country made that a crime which nature never meant to be so.'

Even Parson Woodforde took it in his stride, recording the payments to Moonshine Buck, the smuggler, for cognac, tea and wine.

Pitt brought the business to an end in 1784 by drastically reducing the import duties, but up till that time it was estimated that of the 13,000,000 lbs of tea consumed each year, duty had been paid on only 5,500,000 lbs, the rest having been smuggled.

Marketing
Most of the East India Company's imports were sold at their sales at East India House in Fenchurch Street. Pepper was a

particularly profitable commodity, for it cost 3d a lb in India and was sold in England for 3/- a lb. They also traded in snuff, salt-petre, small pieces of furniture, such as tables and screens, made from exotic woods, cotton cloth, embroidered hangings, ivory, silks, brocades, arrack, spice, cloves, nutmegs, mangoes, carpets and rugs. The Indiamen who went on to China and Japan for tea also brought back porcelain and, in the second half of the century, hand-painted Chinese wallpaper.

The marketing of many of the City's imports took place in the coffee houses. Gresham's Royal Exchange had been destroyed in the fire of 1666 but it was rebuilt and open for business again by 1670 and here for some years merchants would meet and trade their wares 'by sample', the bulk of their goods being stored in the riverside warehouses: but as the coffee houses grew in popularity merchants deserted the Exchange and before long individual coffee houses were associated with different groups of merchants, often providing sale rooms where their commodities could be auctioned.

At Edward Lloyd's coffee house in Tower Street the business of marine insurance developed and eventually grew so large that it moved back to the Royal Exchange. The merchants in the West India trade, which included sugar, rum and coffee, met at the Jerusalem and Garraway's, off Cornhill. The Virginia and Maryland coffee house in Threadneedle Street was the meeting place for merchants interested in the tobacco, sugar and cotton of the southern states of America and close by was the Baltic, where men dealing in the Russian and Baltic trade in timber and tallow did business. In 1744 the Virginia and Maryland joined forces with the Baltic and re-opened as the Virginia and Baltic.

By now their customers were as interested in the ships as their cargoes and met the owners and captains. They were able to check their movements and the amount of cargo space they had available at any given time. For example, a merchant wishing to send tea and coffee he had bought from the East India Company to customers in America might arrange with a captain bringing tallow and grain from the Baltic to reload his ship in London with the tea and coffee and advise the American customers to have ready a cargo of sugar and tobacco which the ship could carry on the return journey to Europe, thereby saving both time and money. In this way the 'shipping market' of the Baltic was established, which soon became as important as the commodity markets.

In 1810 the Virginia and Baltic moved to the Antwerp coffee house in Threadneedle Street and was re-named the Baltic. A few years later the members formed themselves into a club and established a sale room. Tallow was still the most important commodity, but with the end of the century they began dealing in imported wheat. This side of the business almost ceased during the Napoleonic wars and within the next few decades gas-lighting spelt doom to the tallow trade, but by then the repeal of the Corn Laws made for greatly increased imports of grain and the Baltic became the largest market in the country for foreign grain as well as the centre of the world's shipping market.

West Indian merchandise was auctioned by sample at the Jerusalem and Garraway's and before long Garraway's became the most important auction room for many foreign commodities. Bidding in the early days was 'by candle'. The auctioneer lit an inch of candle as a sign for bidding to begin and it continued till the candle had burnt out. In 1722 Defoe mentioned Garraway's as the place 'frequented about noon by people of quality who have business in the City, and the more considerable and wealthy citizens.'

In 1748 there was a disastrous outbreak of fire in Change Alley which destroyed, amongst many other buildings, both the Jerusalem and Garraway's. For the Jerusalem it was the end, but Garraway's was rebuilt and continued to do important business, until the London Commercial Sale Room was opened in Mincing Lane in 1811. This became a general exchange for the wholesale marketing of many commodities which did not have a special exchange of their own. West Indian sugar was its most important market at first, for at this time sugar was Great Britain's most valuable import. It was bought by samples taken from the warehouses and much of it was re-exported. When the East India Company lost its monopoly of trading with the East in 1833 and the business was open to all comers, tea auctions were transferred to Mincing Lane and also the ancient spice market.

It was the foundation of these great wholesale markets, buying for home consumption and also for re-export, which was to bring such wealth and power to the City in the years to come.

With the opening of Georgian times the City of London, with its new Wren churches, was very beautiful, and it was growing fast. Old London Bridge, built in 1209, still stood, as well as the ancient Roman walls and gates, though by now London had spread so far beyond them. The Guildhall, badly damaged in the Great Fire, had been restored by Wren and was once more the meeting place of the Common Council of the City. In 1739 the Mansion House was built as the Lord Mayor's residence, on the site of the old Stocks market, which was moved to Farringdom Street. In the middle years of the century the old houses on London Bridge were removed but the bridge itself remained till the building of Rennie's new bridge began in 1825. The first Westminster Bridge was opened in 1750 and the second City of London bridge was Blackfriars, on which work was begun in 1760, but the first Waterloo bridge was not built till 1811.

Between 1760 and 1766 the walls of the city were pulled down and the gateways removed, but the city boundaries were still clearly defined and within this famous square mile, which was the hub of the country's commerce, the Lord Mayor had the jurisdiction which he still maintains.

Many of the ancient produce markets of the city not only survived but increased in business. Smithfield, by now paved and fenced, was the market for live cattle and sheep, many of which were slaughtered in West Smithfield and sold by the

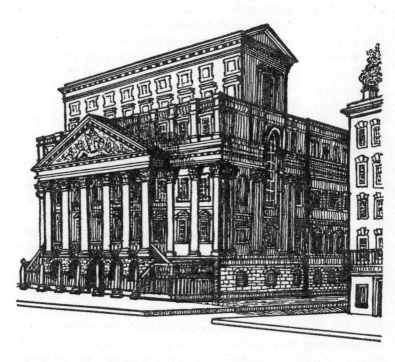

The Mansion House, London, built in 1739

butchers of nearby Newgate market, on the other side of St
Bartholomew's hospital. The animals came from all the home
counties. In the 1750's the livestock from the Duke of Bedford's Woburn estates was sent up to London for sale, instead
of being sent to the cattle markets at Leighton Buzzard or
Luton. The journey took two days and the beasts were fattened
in the fields behind Bedford House in Bloomsbury before being
driven on to Smithfield. In fact the Euston Road was cut about
this time to help the drovers from the north and north-eastern
approaches of London to get their cattle through to Smithfield.

   In the ramshackle sheds and stalls at Billingsgate, the oldest
of all the City produce markets, fish from the Thames was sold

as well as supplies picked up by the bum-boat men from the North Sea fishermen and carried as quickly as possible from the estuary. Leadenhall market close by concentrated by now on poultry and game. The booksellers were to be found mostly around St. Paul's churchyard and Paternoster Row. Here too were the mercers. The Royal Exchange and Ludgate Hill were both famous for their mercers' shops, but as the century wore on and fashionable people tended to live farther west, the milliners, clothiers, drapers and haberdashers moved with them, while into the Royal Exchange moved important institutions such as the Lloyd's Society, the members of which were prepared to insure ships and cargoes on the high seas.

When Covent Garden was an exclusive residential district the streets surrounding it were famous for their shops selling clothing of all descriptions. In Bedford Street and Russell Street, Henrietta Street and Chandos Street you could buy silks, satins, brocades, velvets, gold and silver braid, silver buttons and the finest English cloth. In the midst of it all the ancient fruit and vegetable market, unabashed by the elegance and dignity of the houses which surrounded it, spread over more and more of the piazza.

When fashion moved still farther west, into Mayfair and Belgravia, Bond Street and St James's Street were the places to shop. The Civet Cat in New Bond Street was famous for its perfumes and cosmetics, Richard Robinson's shop for its exotic confectionery, while James Lock, the St James's Street hatter, who took over the business from his father-in-law in 1759, remains London's most distinguished hatter to this day.

By the beginning of the nineteenth century, London stretched from Bethnal Green in the east to Mayfair and Westminster in the west, and from Islington in the north to Newington Butts and Bermondsey in the south.

It was at this time that the West India docks on the Isle of Dogs were built, and the hoists and winches installed for unloading great blocks of mahogany were one of the sights of the town. The docks at Wapping, the Surrey docks, the East India docks and St Katharine's dock soon followed and the stage was set for the great Victorian boom.

The population of London had risen to well over a million, representing something like fourteen per cent of the entire population of England and Wales.

Covent Garden market in the 18th century

Chapter Eight

TRANSPORT

Roads

Many factors contributed to the transformation of England from the self-contained, slow-moving rural land of the early eighteenth century to the highly industrialised country of the nineteenth, and one of them was the change in the methods of communication and transport.

At the beginning of this time roads were so bad in many parts of the country that it was difficult even to ride a horse on them. Whole districts were inevitably isolated from the main stream of the nation's life. Counties were still called 'countries' and the Lord Lieutenants and local magistrates, who ruled the immediate destinies of the people in their areas, were of far more significance to them than the government far away in London, whose main concern was for foreign affairs and the acquisition and maintenance of new lands or trading stations abroad, where independent merchants could extend our commerce and bring wealth back to the country.

The government did not accept responsibility for the welfare of the ordinary people. Law and order, the care of the aged, the treatment of the sick and help for those who were unemployed or disabled were undertaken, if at all, by the parish, usually augmented by benevolent institutions founded by local benefactors.

Least of all did the government take the initiative in providing proper roads. Each section of a road was the responsibility of the parish through which it passed. A surveyor of roads was appointed by the magistrates for each parish and it was his duty to see that local residents with property above a certain value provided six days of labour free each year for their maintenance. Usually the surveyor hired workmen for the job and collected the money from the rate-payers, but most people resented having to pay for the upkeep of roads on which travellers living perhaps miles away happened to pass. The result was that the roads fell into a deplorable state and it was not till the Turnpike Trusts that matters began to improve.

These Trusts were formed by groups of people who took control of certain stretches of road and kept them in good repair, obtaining money for the work by charging a toll to the users, which was collected by the toll keepers who guarded the toll gates. Each Trust was legalised by a separate Act of Parliament and throughout the eighteenth century hundreds were passed.

Very gradually harder and better roads were built but over and over again we read of complaints about the roads. Henry Purefroy, writing to Bath in August, 1742, despairs of ever reaching there that year, with the autumn approaching, for 'I am afraid the Roads will be bad', and two years later, writing to a shopkeeper in Brackley, he thanks him for mending the road but says 'there is since that a quick sand in the lane that my coachman with his coach horse was like to be mired in it as hee will tell you, and that prevents me from coming to Brackley.'

Mrs Purefroy in a letter to her nephew who is coming to stay instructs him that: 'The Ailesbury stage coach goes out from the Bell Inne in Holborn every Tuesday at 6 in ye morning and comes to Ailesbury that night, next day it comes to the Lord Cobham's Arms in Buckingham and there our Coach may meet you. But how you get from Shalstone to Northampton I know not . . . neither do I know whether that is the road to Lincoln or no.'

During the 1760's Mr Cole often rode because the roads round Bletchley were too bad to travel in his chaise, and when he moved into Cambridgeshire most of his furniture went by

Paying a toll at a turn-pike. The turn-pikes were the barriers put across the roads

river from Bedford. There was even delay in getting it as far as the river 'on account of the roads'.

Riders often found it easier to avoid the roads and travel over the fields, but with increasing enclosures this practice was not always possible. Horses were expensive and people walked very long distances on foot. John Metcalf, the road-maker, better known as Blind Jack of Knaresborough, once re-fused the offer of a seat in the London to York coach, saying that he preferred to walk, and the coach was so delayed by floods and other hazards of the road that he actually arrived ahead of it.

Travellers sometimes bought a horse for a journey and sold it when they arrived at their destination, but it was unwise to walk or travel on one's own, for the roads were infested with highwaymen and it was still easy to lose one's way, for only the main roads were signposted.

Of the road from Preston to Wigan, Arthur Young wrote in 1770: 'I know not in the whole range of the language, terms sufficiently expressive to describe this infernal road . . . let me most seriously caution all travellers who may accidentally pur-pose to travel this terrible country to avoid it as they would the devil; for a thousand to one but they break their neck or their limbs by overthrows or breaking down. They will meet here with ruts, which I actually measured four feet deep . . . I passed three carts broken down in these eighteen miles of execrable memory.'

Coaches

Pack horse trains and the carriers' carts were still the only way of transporting heavy goods on land and the public coach services were available for those who preferred them to riding, though the journeys were very slow and uncomfortable. In the middle years of the century the run from London to Buckingham took a day and the fare was ten shillings. London to Edinburgh took ten days and London to Bath two days. In 1754 an inn in Manchester advertised that 'A Flying Coach, however incredible it may appear, will actually, barring accidents, arrive in London in Four Days and a half, after leaving Manchester.'

Stage coaches, drawn by two or four horses, were similar to those first built in the seventeenth century and very little different from private travelling coaches. They were a little lighter than those of Queen Anne's time but still had no springs. A guard armed with a blunderbuss always accompanied the coach, as a protection against attack.

A stage coach of the mid-18th century

An inside seat was more expensive and considerably more comfortable in winter time, unless you were prone to sickness. Outside passengers sat on the roof or in a basket between the back wheels. A visitor from Germany in 1782 found himself in a seat on top of the London to Leicester coach. 'The machine rolled along with prodigious rapidity over the stones through the town and every moment we seemed to fly into the air,' he wrote . . . . 'This continual fear of death at last became insupportable to me, and therefore, no sooner were we crawling up a rather steep hill, and consequently proceeding slower than usual, than I carefully crept from the top of the coach, and was lucky enough to get myself snugly ensconced in the basket behind.'

Nothing good came of the move for shortly afterwards it began to rain and he was soaked to the skin.

In the 1780's, just before the outbreak of the French Revolution, John Palmer designed a new type of coach in which the body was suspended on springs. He inaugurated a regular coach service from London to the more important towns and obtained the government concession for carrying the mail. John Palmer's mail coaches were faster, but, at least in the early days, no more comfortable. 'I had the most disagreeable journey owing to the new improved patent coach,' wrote Matthew Bolton in 1787, after a journey from London to Exeter, 'a vehicle loaded with iron trappings and the greatest complication of unmechanical contrivances jumbled together that I have ever witnessed.'

He became very ill and had to stop at Axminster and go to bed. When he arrived at Exeter the landlady at his inn told him that 'the passengers who arrived every night were in general so ill that they were obliged to go supperless to bed.'

However, both roads and the mail coaches did improve and by 1830 the run from London to Edinburgh was taking only 46 hours, to Manchester eighteen hours and Bath fourteen hours. Stage coaches had reached a speed of eight miles an hour with occasional bursts of eleven to twelve miles an hour and

A post-chaise, 1725

people were becoming concerned about the strain on the horses. 'We see frequently from ten to fourteen and even sixteen persons on the top of a stage . . .' wrote one protester. 'The weight of these, together with the vast quantity of luggage stowed in every part, and the massy vehicle capable of supporting such a weight is far too much for four horses at the rate they are forced to go.'

These were the great coaching days, when inns both in London and along the main roads bustled and prospered and offered gargantuan meals to cold and hungry travellers. By 1828 forty coaches were travelling each day to Brighton, the most popular being the famous 'Comet', in which young bucks could make the journey from London in only six hours.

Private Coaches

For private owners there were heavier coaches for long distances and lighter ones for use in London and elsewhere, where the roads were better. The post chaise was popular and comfortable for long journeys. The body hung by leather braces to upright springs. The back wheels were considerably larger than the front wheels and luggage could be stacked both in front and behind. Horses were changed at each posting house on the journey.

A phaeton for two drawn by two horses was the smart thing towards the end of the century. The perch phaeton, with the

A phaeton, early 19th century

body immediately over the front wheels was a sporting and rather dangerous design, but the landau, introduced about the middle of the century, was like the older type of coach or chariot, except that the upper part could be opened and pulled back.

The gig, drawn by one horse, had only two wheels, the open body being suspended by leather braces from curved springs. A two-horse gig was known as a curricle, and if it had a hood it was a cabriolet. Another form, with a different arrangement of springs, was called a whisky.

Sedan Chairs

Sedan chairs were used in London and other towns and cities during the eighteenth century, mainly by ladies of fashion to protect their delicate skirts from the muddy streets, but as conditions improved and light carriages became more practicable, Sedan chairs fell into disuse.

Road Making

Arguments on the best ways of road-making were long and took some strange turns, one theorist advocating: 'Remove the obstructions, clean the ditches, let in the sun and air, and the roads will grow better of themselves.'

First of the British road-makers was General Wade, who, after the 1715 Jacobite rebellion, set his men to repairing some

A sedan chair. Early 18th century

of the roads in the Highlands, by removing boulders and generally levelling. Blind Jack of Knaresborough built many miles of roads across the hills and mountains of northern England during the 1760's and 1770's, but it was John McAdam (1756–1836) of Ayrshire who, after being appointed trustee of the roads in his own parish, made the first fundamental improvements. Hitherto ruts had been filled in with gravel, which meant that the surface quickly became uneven again, but McAdam advocated the use of small fragments of broken stone, which the weight of passing vehicles would press down to a hard, smooth surface.

Thomas Telford (1757–1834) went farther than this. He saw the need for a strong base, for which he used close-set stone pavement. Small stones laid over this were compressed by the traffic into a solid and serviceable road. Early in the nineteenth century Telford was made responsible for the building of many roads in Britain. He selected the most practical routes and gradients for the horses and their heavy loads and in re-making old roads he very often dug down to the Roman foundations and built the whole road anew. For paved streets he used a twelve-inch layer of broken stones covered with gravel and overlaid with gravel or limestone paving slabs. Roads were built with a camber, the foundation stones being larger in the middle than at the sides. These were covered by a six-inch layer of stones which were broken down to an approximately uniform size, small enough to pass through a two and a half inch ring. Where stone was in short supply, broken stones or gravel and pebbles might be used, in a layer which was about sixteen inches thick at the crown of the road and ten inches thick on either side.

Bridges

Telford was also a bridge-builder and built many of the bridges carried by his roads over rivers and canals. He also rebuilt some of the existing bridges.

Canals

Carriage by water was still the most practical method for heavy transport and before the first canals were built the beds of a number of rivers had been scoured and deepened in order to accommodate larger boats for increasing distances inland.

The story of the British canals is inseparable from that of the development of our heavy industries. When Brindley's first canal, of only seven miles, was put into operation, the cost of

The Menai bridge, built by Telford. 1819–1826

transport of the Duke of Bridgewater's coal was reduced to less than half and, as we have seen, within the next few years, until the coming of the railways, canals were built all over the country, solving for a while the problem of the transport of heavy, imperishable goods. The vast army of workmen engaged in the excavation and building of these canals came to be called the inland navigators or 'navvies'.

Ships

During the long voyages undertaken by the armoured ships of the East India Company, British sailors developed their skill in navigation. The Company's fleet of sturdy, oak, three-masted sailing ships was, in fact, a private navy, and during the Seven Years War they carried troops to India for the government.

At the beginning of the seventeenth century there had been thirty of these vessels in service, each of about 1,000 tons, and as the art of shipbuilding developed they grew bigger and stronger and their tonnage doubled.

The ships of the Royal Navy were similar, but in 1719 the Navy Board laid down a fixed scale of dimensions and tonnage for ships of every class, which remained in force for nearly a century, so that there was no great development in basic design during the eighteenth century. The *Royal George,* launched in 1756, carried a hundred guns and her tonnage was 2047. Nelson's *Victory*, built in 1775, was one of the fastest sailing ships of the day, yet it differed little from the *Royal George* and the effective range of her guns was only 1200 yards.

By 1837, though the Navy possessed a few steam warships, life on board had changed little since Nelson's time. There was no regular uniform for ordinary seamen. The press gangs were still operating and discipline was maintained by flogging. The Admiralty did not favour steamships and the Royal Navy's largest vessel, carrying 110 guns, was entirely under sail, shorter but a few feet wider than the *Victory*, which had by now been in service for over sixty years.

Even the races on the China run between the slim, tall Baltimore tea clippers and the cumbersome old English windjammers were not to take place till the 1840's.

Nelson's flag-ship The Victory, *built in 1775 and still in service when Queen Victoria came to the throne*

Chapter Nine

EDUCATION

Throughout the eighteenth century the government took no responsibility for education, and as the population increased the facilities for free education which had been provided by wealthy benefactors of earlier centuries became quite inadequate. By 1837 only about one in ten of the population went to school and half the people of London could not read or write. Yet, paradoxically, Georgian England, for all its haphazard and uneven education, produced a very high proportion of men of outstanding intellect.

The Public Schools

Amongst the upper classes some boys were still taught at home by tutors, many of whom were Huguenot refugees, but an increasing number were sent away to the fashionable schools, notably Eton, Harrow, Winchester, Rugby and Westminster. Most of these schools had originally been grammar school foundations for the free education of the sons of local men, but as prices rose and certain headmasters found that their statutes allowed them to admit a certain number of fee-paying students, to augment their own small salaries, the practice of charging fees grew. Eton had attracted the nobility for many years. In the old days boys had lived out in the town, in expensive lodgings, usually with their tutors. Now the house system was established within the school and a far stricter discipline was maintained. Harrow became fashionable in early Georgian times and by 1718 had 104 fee-paying

students compared with 40 free scholars. The segration between the rich and poor in these schools was rigid. At Eton
only peers could be top of a form and at Winchester the young
Duke of Hamilton, as the senior in rank, became automatically
head of the school.

It was not long before the misnamed 'public' schools became
almost entirely fee-paying. The education was adapted to the
needs of the boys. There were not many masters and most
pupils still had their own tutors. Latin was the principle subject but Greek and English literature were usually taught,
and French, dancing and fencing were available for those
who wanted to learn them. There were no organized games
and in their spare time the boys were left very much to their
own devices. They played cricket amongst themselves but
football was regarded as a vulgar sport. There was a certain
amount of flogging but most of it seems to have been inflicted
by the older boys upon the younger ones, whom they used
as fags. There is little evidence of cruelty on the part of the
staff.

Harrow school in the 18th century. (Viewed from the east)

Students at Oxford, 1814

Oxford and Cambridge

Most of these boys moved on to Oxford or Cambridge, where the educational standards had sunk to a deplorably low level. Dissenters and Roman Catholics were still barred from the Universities and apart from the few poor students who went up on scholarships, usually to study for the Church, and who were in many ways socially segregated, Oxford and Cambridge were regarded as pleasant clubs.

Unlike the Scottish universities, where the prestige of the medical school at Edinburgh, for example, was already high, the English universities had almost ceased to be seats of learning and their numbers fell to half those of the seventeenth century.

At Oxford, Classics was the principal subject and throughout the eighteenth century examinations were a routine of question and answer which a student could learn in advance. Cambridge was little better, though they had instituted the mathematical tripos, for those who cared to sit for it.

Endowments for professorships had deteriorated in value and dons were ill-paid. They gave very few lectures and tuition was mainly by individual tutors.

Movements for reform did not begin till the end of the century. In 1800 a written and oral B.A. examination was established at Oxford and by 1824 Cambridge students could sit for the Classical tripos as well as the mathematical tripos, but it was many years before they regained their academic prestige.

The Grand Tour

The sons of wealthy families usually made the 'Grand Tour' of France and Italy after leaving the university. For some this was little more than routine sight-seeing but for others it was a valuable education, during which they improved their French and Italian, polished their manners and widened their outlook. A fair proportion of students went to the Middle Temple after the university, for a legal training.

Grammar Schools

Many of the old grammar schools which had already begun to decay after the Restoration deteriorated still further during the eighteenth century. As prices rose endowments became so inadequate that there were not enough funds for proper staffing. By 1795 Lord Chief Justice Kenyon declared that most of the ancient grammar schools had become 'empty walls, without scholars and everything neglected but the receipt of salaries.' In some cases headmasters corruptly pocketed the bulk of the money available and employed a half-educated, inadequate master to do the work.

Dissenting Academies

A large number of fee-paying day and boarding schools, run by private proprietors, came into existence at this time, some very good, some tolerable, but all too many nearly as bad as Mr. Squeers' Dotheboys Hall.

It was the academies first opened by the Dissenters early in the eighteenth century which helped to fill many of the serious gaps in the Georgian educational system. They catered mainly for the middle classes of prosperous traders and merchants and the education they provided was far more suitable for the practical demands of the dawning Industrial Revolution than the traditional teaching of the public schools and universities. Their curricula included science, mathematics and geography, as well as the classics and living languages.

Many of the Dissenting Academies were so successful that Anglicans sent their sons to them, and towards the end of the century some of the fashionable schools, such as Oundle and Rugby, copied them. Warrington Academy equipped boys for the learned professions and Philip Doddridge's Academy at Northampton and the schools at Kendal and Hackney were all very popular.

Middle class boys and younger sons of small squires were often apprenticed on leaving school to merchants, bankers, apothecaries, attorneys and brewers, paying premiums of anything from £20 to £100. Premiums rose during the century and by 1800 some London merchants were asking as much as £1,000 to apprentice a boy.

Charity Schools

For the steadily increasing numbers of the working classes there were very few chances of education and most of them

A Charity School in the early 19th century

grew up illiterate. There were dame schools for small children and schools for the older ones which were little better. The charge was anything from 4d to 9d a week and they were run by half-literate men and women who were often looking after a small shop or business at the same time. There were no standards. Anyone could open a school and set up as a teacher. It was said, in fact, that 'their only qualification for this employment was their unfitness for every other'.

There was a growing desire for education, yet many people could not afford even the few pence that this minimum of learning cost.

From the end of the seventeenth century the Society for the Propagation of the Gospel had run a few charity schools, their aim being 'to combat Popery and to teach the children of the poor to keep their stations'. By 1714 there were 5,000 children attending charity schools in London and about 20,000 throughout the country. They were clothed and afterwards apprenticed to a trade. Throughout the eighteenth century the

The Foundling Hospital, London, founded by Sir Thomas Coram in 1739

Charity School movement spread and both Dissenters and the Church of England opened schools where reading, writing and arithmetic were taught, with spinning and knitting for the girls.

Though ostensibly humanitarian, the main purpose of providing this education was still to train the children in the habit of subordination and acceptance of their lowly lot. To quote Isaac Watts, they were taught 'to know what their station in life is, how mean their circumstances, how necessary 'tis for them to be diligent, laborious, honest and faithful, humble and submissive, what duties they owe to the rest of mankind and particularly to their superiors.'

In 1739 Thomas Coram endowed the Foundling Hospital in London, where abandoned children were given a home and education, but it was a rule that they should not be educated to as high a standard as those who had parents.

Boys were apprenticed to a trade. Most of the girls were put to domestic service, a few being apprenticed to dressmakers.

Sunday Schools

In 1780 Robert Raikes founded the first Sunday School at Gloucester. This was intended for the very poor child factory workers who had no time during the week to attend any school. Sunday was their only free day, during which they were apt to run wild, so that farmers and others complained of the damage done to their property. Robert Raikes' Sunday Schools attracted large numbers of children and also their parents. They would walk miles to attend them, carrying their Sunday dinners with them, and spend all day learning the three R's and receiving religious instruction, so that five years later Raikes was able to write with pleasure of their 'sense of sub-ordination and of due respect to their superiors.'

British and Foreign Schools Society and the National Schools

A few years later Joseph Lancaster founded a school in Southwark where some hundred boys and girls were taught reading, writing and arithmetic for about 4d a week and it was so successful that by 1814 it had led to the formation of the British and Foreign School Society. The schools of this society taught Christianity but were non-sectarian and the Church of England soon formed a rival society, the National Society for promoting the Education of the Poor in the Principles of the Established Church.

By this time many theories were being expounded in regard to education in general and that of the poor in particular. At first the official view of the government was that it would be 'prejudicial to their morals and happiness; it would teach them to despise their lot in life.'

However, the revolution in France was a stern warning to those who underestimated the intelligence and potential power of the working classes. From the attitude that education might do a great deal of harm, 'as it would enable them to read everything that would tend to inflame their passions', there was a change to the point of view that 'ignorance might give birth to disastrous eruptions'. The idea now was to teach them a little, explain that their place in life had been ordained by an inscrutable Providence, and instil in them a sweet reasonableness. A little education, it was thought, would form 'many beneficial habits of an indelible nature; habits of sub-mission and respect for their superiors', and religion would teach obedience.

It was many years before the government would act. In 1818 the Lord Brougham Commission reported that of the 130,000 parishes in England, 3,500 had no school at all and only 3,000 had an endowed school of any kind. The Charity School move-ment had hardly scratched the surface of the problem for probably not more than 40,000 children passed through their hands each year.

In 1833 the government made its first, half-hearted gesture with a grant of £20,000 for school building. If a district could raise half the necessary amount for a building the government would supply the other half, and the funds were to be adminis-tered by the National Society, which had the bulk of the money, and the British and Foreign Schools Society.

In 1837 Lord Brougham declared in the House of Lords that England had 'done less for the Education of the People than any one of the more civilized countries of the world.'

London University

Apart from this elementary and still very rudimentary education, for which the recommended salary for teachers was £23 a year, with a maximum training of five months, there was still no provision for University education for those who were not members of the Church of England.

In 1828 the secular University College in Gower Street was founded, where the curriculum included languages, mathe-matics, history, political economy and science, the money having been raised by Jeremy Bentham and his circle. The Church of England disapproved of this 'godless institution in Gower Street' and three years later opened King's College in the Strand, but by 1836 the University of London was created, including both colleges. The new university had the right to confer degrees and within the next few years several more universities and colleges were founded throughout the country.

*A small girl being taught
by her governess.
Late 18th century*

The Education of Girls

Women had been relegated to a position of social inferiority during the Commonwealth and by the eighteenth century the general attitude towards the education of girls was still that, on the whole, they got on better without it.

Amongst the wealthy, girls were taught at home by governesses. They learnt to read and write, to sew and cook. Sometimes they learnt a little French or Italian and could play a musical instrument. In Georgian times this would probably have been the piano, which had been invented in Italy in 1709 and gradually supplanted the spinet and the harpsichord.

Early in the eighteenth century marriages amongst the wealthy were usually a business arrangement and parents argued that prospective husbands distrusted and disliked educated and intellectual women, while men often declared that if a woman were educated she would not be so amenable and obedient.

The Royal ladies of the Georgian courts did not help matters and intellect was regarded as an unfeminine and unfashionable attribute, to be deplored.

There had been many protests during the seventeenth century about this attitude and there were some notable rebels during the eighteenth century. Lady Mary Wortley Montagu, who flouted convention by making a run-away marriage for love, was constantly extolling the delights of education to her daughter and grand-daughter, though she warned them 'that a woman would be wise to conceal any learning she attains'.

In the 1760's Mrs. Montague established the Blue Stocking Club at her home in Portman Square and here met a distinguished and intellectual circle of men and women, including Elizabeth Carter, Mrs. Vesey, Hannah More, Fanny Burney, Dr. Johnson, James Boswell, Horace Walpole and William Wilberforce. Mrs. Carter, in particular, was astonishingly erudite. Dr. Johnson, one of her admirers, said that: 'A man is in general better pleased when he has a good dinner on his table than when his wife talks Greek. My old friend, Mrs. Carter, could make a pudding as well as translate Epictetus from the Greek and work a handkerchief as well as compose a poem.'

However, the accomplishments of these few outstanding women who, in the main, had educated themselves, did not influence the general attitude towards the education of girls, at least for many years to come. In 1787 Mary Wollstonecraft published her *Thoughts on the Education of Daughters,* in which she pleaded that men should be content with rational fellowship instead of slavish obedience: and after Burke had published his *Vindication of the Rights of Man* she replied with her *Vindication of the Rights of Women,* but most people were horrified and even the good Hannah More called her a 'disgusting and unnatural character.'

By the early years of the nineteenth century Jane Austen was echoing Lady Montagu's words of more than half a century earlier. 'A woman . . . if she has the misfortune to know anything, should conceal it as well as she can.'

There were no schools for girls to compare with the public schools, the best of the grammar schools or the Dissenting

Academies for boys, but towards the end of the eighteenth century boarding schools became fashionable, where girls were taught a little French and English, arithmetic and geography, as well as needlework and dancing. By the early nineteenth century the number of these schools had increased but the quality of the education was still very low.

For girls whose parents could afford neither a boarding school nor a governess, but who were above the social class for which the Charity Schools catered, there was hardly any means of acquiring an education, unless their mothers were able to teach them.

Chapter Ten

CRIME AND PUNISHMENT

At the beginning of Georgian times justice in England was administered as it had been since medieval times, by unpaid Justices of the Peace. These men were chosen from amongst the local gentry, by the Lord Lieutenant of the county, to govern their district for the Crown. Their duties included the levying of the county rate, the maintenance of roads and bridges, the licensing of taverns, the administration of the Poor Law, and the supervision of houses of correction or 'bridewells', prisons and workhouses. They administered either at the quarter and petty sessions or from their own homes.

Constables, whose task it was to help the magistrates and maintain law and order, were also unpaid citizens who took yearly terms of office in rotation.

Justices of the Peace were allowed certain fees for expenses, but it was not till 1792 that stipendiary magistrates with regular incomes were instituted. In the country districts men of integrity and honour could usually be found to fulfil the duties required of them, but in the large towns and London there was a growing tendency to corruption. The punishments the magistrates had the power to wield were severe, and prisoners with means were only too thankful when they found judges who were open to bribery. These 'trading justices', whom Smollett described as of 'profligate lives, needy, mean, ignorant and rapacious', managed to bribe their way into office and many made handsome livings.

A 'Charlie' – a paid watchman of the early 18th century

137

The system of voluntary constables also broke down, for men often delegated their duties, for a small sum of money, to those who were prepared to do the work for a living. As early as Charles II's time these watchmen, known as Charlies, had already become an institution. They were usually too old for any other kind of work, and being armed only with long staves they were useless against strong and well-armed criminals.

In 1748 Henry Fielding was appointed magistrate for Westminster and Middlesex and later chairman of the quarter sessions for Westminster. He moved into a house in Bow Street with his blind half-brother John, who was soon to succeed him.

Crime in London was on the increase and the government asked Henry Fielding to submit a plan to combat it. The scheme he devised developed into the organization of the Bow Street runners, which Sir John administered after Henry's early death. At first there were only six runners, but they were men with special skill in solving crimes and they were prepared to travel anywhere in the country, or even abroad, where their help was needed. In addition to this 'special branch' John Fielding had a patrol of sixty-eight men based on the Bow Street office. They were divided into thirteen parties, each comprising an officer and three or four men, and they patrolled the streets at night and at other times when there were large gatherings which might break into disorder. They were all armed with cutlasses and the officers also carried a brace of pistols. They did not wear a special uniform until the uniformed Horse Patrol, which was formed early in the nineteenth century to guard the roads against a fresh outbreak of highway robbery, came into existence. Then the Bow Street men were put into dark blue coats and trousers, red waistcoats and black leather hats, and were known as the Robin Redbreasts.

The Bow Street patrols operated for nearly seventy years, till the formation of Sir Robert Peel's police force in 1829, by

A Bow Street runner of the 18th and early 19th century

which time many more mounted and foot patrols were coming into operation all over the country, based on local police offices.

There were never more than twelve Bow Street runners and usually there were only eight. They did not wear a special uniform and Townshend, one of the most famous, who often used to guard George III when he was Prince of Wales, was famous for his wide-brimmed, white hat and loud suits. The insignia of office was a small baton surmounted by a crown and, like the patrols, they were armed.

The Criminals

As late as 1769 there were a hundred and sixty offences for which the penalty was death by hanging. Magistrates were often merciful and found loopholes in the law, but during the early years of the eighteenth century an average of twenty people were hanged each year in London alone, some for such small crimes as the theft of a few shillings.

Public hangings were regarded by many as a free entertainment and it was not till the middle years of the nineteenth century that, with a growing distaste for such morbid cruelty, the practise was stopped.

Smuggling, highway robbery, horse and cattle thieving all carried the death penalty. People were imprisoned for debt and stayed there till the money was paid or they had died from want and neglect or gaol fever. Worse still, they were committed to prison before trial and often had to wait for months before their cases were heard.

There were prisons in nearly every town and there were about two hundred county gaols, nominally under the control of the sheriffs, but in practice governed by despotic gaolers. Prisons were often attached to the houses of correction which had been instituted in Tudor times to house vagrants, who were supposed to earn their keep by some useful employment, but people committed to prisons, apart from the debtors, were usually there for a relatively short period, awaiting either trial or death.

The prisons were terrible places, without light, sanitation, ventilation or heat. Prisoners awaiting trial were expected to provide their own food. They bought what they could afford from the gaolers. Otherwise they subsisted on charity and sometimes were allowed into the streets, in chained gangs, to beg for their bread. Prisoners awaiting death were supplied with a minimum of food by the magistrates.

John Howard, who became High Sheriff of Bedfordshire during the reign of George III, visited Bedford gaol and was shocked to find that the warders were unpaid, relying on money extorted from the prisoners for their own subsistence. This money included a 'gaol delivery' fee which acquitted prisoners were forced to pay before they were set free. Howard reported what he had found to a committee of the House of Commons and spent most of the remaining years of his life pleading for reform in the treatment of prisoners, but he received little practical support and it was not till many years after his death, in 1790, that some of his ideas were eventually adopted.

Very early in his career of crime Jonathan Wild found himself in the debtors' prison in Wood Street off Cheapside, and as he had no money at all he was relegated to the worst of three alternative accommodations, the Hole, where, in a room thirty feet long by fifteen feet wide, seventy men and women debtors cooked, ate and slept. The beds were bare wooden shelves ranged round the walls, the highest of which were reached by ladders.

It was in 1739 that Dick Turpin, the most notorious of all the Georgian highwaymen, bought himself a new coat and shoes and, followed by five mourners whom he had hired for the occasion and presented with black hatbands and gloves, took his last ride in the death cart from the prison courtyard at York castle to the gallows outside the city gates.

The alternative to hanging was transportation to the American colonies, and lesser crimes were punished by fines, floggings or exposure in the stocks. With the loss of America in 1776 transportation had to stop for a while and prisoners were sent to the rotting hulks of ancient sailing ships, too

Stand and Deliver!
A highwayman of the
18th century

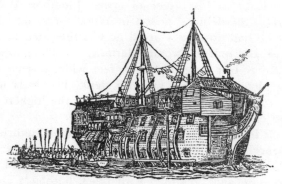

A prison hulk at Portsmouth in the 1780's

old for any other service, which were moored at Woolwich, Portsmouth, Plymouth and other seaports. The prisoners were put ashore from these each day, to do hard labour in the neighbourhood, and herded back at night time.

However, Captain Cook had recently discovered Australia and by 1788 the earliest settlement in New South Wales, Port Jackson, was founded as a penal settlement. Transportation now began to Australia and was to continue till early Victorian times. In England prison conditions grew worse, for while the growing spirit of humanitarianism was strong enough for the number of offences carrying the death penalty to be greatly reduced, the prisons became more crowded than ever, with unfortunate prisoners awaiting the alternative fate, which was transportation.

The main debtors' prisons in London, the Marshalsea and the Fleet, were a national disgrace, despite an increasing number of protests. Dartmoor prison was built during the Napoleonic wars to house French prisoners of war, and only ten years after it was put into use it was described as a 'great tomb of the living.' It was not used for criminal detention until 1850.

Newgate prison had been burnt to the ground during the Gordon riots in 1780, but had been rebuilt on a similar pattern.

Newgate prison in 1800, where Elizabeth Fry began her prison visiting

Here it was that the Quaker, Elizabeth Fry, began her prison visiting during the last years of the Regency and throughout the remaining years of the Georgian period.

She found eight hundred and twenty-two prisoners crowded into the Newgate cells, more than three hundred of them women with young children. These women prisoners had nothing to do to pass their time. They cooked, washed and slept on the stone floors of their cells, living lives of hopeless depravity. Most were awaiting trial and transportation or death.

Elizabeth Fry devoted herself to their welfare. She organized a system of prison visitors and together they not only held prayer meetings and Bible readings but provided the women with clothing and the means of keeping themselves clean, as well as materials with which they could sew, knit and spin, to earn a little money and establish a measure of self-respect.

She made it her business to travel by coach to the ports of embarkation of the transportation ships and visit each prison ship before it sailed: and she did what she could to comfort those left behind to face the gallows. She and her husband visited prisons all over the country and also in Europe, pleading for and gradually achieving more humane treatment for the inmates.

These were the years of the Methodist revival which had been founded in mid-Georgian times by John and Charles Wesley. The Wesleys and John Whitfield had all begun their preaching careers as missionaries of the S.P.C.K. in the American colonies and also devoted time to visiting prisons in London and the provinces. The Wesleys founded the Methodist movement. Whitfield differed from them on minor points of doctrine and continued as an independent evangelist.

There were many movements at this time to try to relieve the trials of the poor, but they were all hampered by those in positions of wealth and authority who still regarded them as a race apart, unprivileged by Divine decree.

Chapter Eleven

THE ARTS AND ENTERTAINMENT

Newspapers

During the eighteenth century four-page newspapers, printed on hand-presses, were being published, and by the 1770's many devoted about half their space to reporting Parliamentary debates.

There were several dailies in London and many provincial towns and cities had their own newspapers, usually weeklies. The first Sunday paper appeared in 1780 and *The Times* in 1785, under the name of the *Daily Universal Register*. It was printed in sixteen columns on a double sheet, and by the end of the century its daily circulation had risen to 4,800. The *Morning Post* was probably second in popularity. It was first published in 1795 and by 1800 its circulation was 2,000 a day.

After 1814 steam presses were used and the size and scope of newspapers greatly increased, their circulation growing very quickly.

Literature

At the beginning of the eighteenth century the legal restriction on the permitted number of printing presses was abolished, with the result that more printing and publishing firms came into existence and many more books were written.

Publishing became a profitable business and although a number of authors of learned works still relied on financial support from rich patrons, professional writers were now able to make an independent living of sorts. By the 1740's there were circulating libraries in London and the more fashionable provincial centres and poetry, travels, belle lettres and novels all found avid readers.

Early in the eighteenth century Richard Steele and Joseph Addison founded the *Spectator* and the *Tatler*, Daniel Defoe published *Robinson Crusoe* and Dean Swift *Gulliver's Travels*. Later Dr Johnson compiled his dictionary while Boswell collected the material for his great biography.

Richardson, Sterne, Fielding, Smollett and Oliver Goldsmith were the important novelists of the eighteenth century. Blake, Cowper and Burns were working during the later years and Sir Walter Scott and Jane Austen belong to the early years of the nineteenth century, during which there was a tremendous outpouring of incomparable English prose and poetry, Words-

A circulating library of the early 19th century

worth, Southey, Coleridge, Charles Lamb, William Hazlitt, Thomas de Quincey, Keats, Shelley, Byron, Thomas Hood all reflecting a romantic revival from the materialism of much of the eighteenth century and the rebellion against economic and political oppression.

Children's Literature

Up till the nineteenth century there was little children's literature. For the very young, there were the nursery stories of good and bad fairies, witches, giants and monsters, and the moral tale of *Goody Two-Shoes*. In 1740 *Tommy Thumb's Song Book* and *Instruction and Amusement of Little Master Tommy and Pretty Miss Polly* were published, but the first children's books of real literary merit were not written till Charles and Mary Lamb's contributions to William Godwin's Juvenile Library. *Tales from Shakespeare* appeared in 1807, *Mrs. Leicester's School* the same year, and *Poetry for Children* two years later.

With the rationalism of the nineteenth century came controversy on the wisdom of training a child's imagination and literary taste on fantasies and fiction. Charles Lamb was one of the first to deplore the tendency of some of the educationists to decry fantasy in children's stories in favour of stark instruction and unimaginative realism.

'Knowledge must now come to a child *in the shape of knowledge,*' he wrote to Coleridge, 'and his empty noddle must be turned with conceit of his own powers when he has learnt that a horse is an animal, and Billy is better than a horse, and such like; instead of that beautiful interest in wild tales which made the child a man while all the time he suspected himself to be no bigger than a child. Science has succeeded to poetry no less in the little walks of children than with men. Is there no possibility of averting this sore evil? Think of what you would have been now, if instead of being fed with tales and old wives' fables in childhood, you had been crammed with geography and natural history?'

This outburst was prompted by an announcement by the publisher, John Marshall, that his children's books had been 'entirely divested of that prejudicial nonsense (to young minds), the Tales of Hobgoblins, Witches, Fairies, Love, Gallantry, etc.' Mrs Trimmer and Mrs Barbauld, two high-minded writers for the young, agreed with Marshall that fairies and the like were so much superstitious rubbish. Lamb was infuriated. 'Damn them!' he said. 'I mean the cursed Barbauld crew, those blights and blasts of all that is human in man and child.'

Artists

Of the eighteenth century artists, William Hogarth is outstanding, not only because, in the words of E. V. Lucas, he was 'the first great natural British painter, the first man to look at the English life around him like an Englishman and paint it without affectation or foreign influence', but because he was the first to make pictures popular amongst all ranks of society, for he was also an engraver, and he sold the engravings of his own works at a price which made them available to the ordinary public.

Amongst those who could afford to buy original pictures, there was still a taste for portraits, often against a classical background. In the 1760's Joshua Reynolds was at the height of his popularity. Thomas Gainsborough moved from his native Suffolk to Bath, to paint the fashionable visitors, and then to London, where he set up his studio in Pall Mall. Romney arrived in London in 1762 and settled in Cavendish Square. Angelica Kauffman reached London in 1766 and soon established herself, at her house in Golden Square, as one of the most fashionable artists in Town and a friend of Sir Joshua Reynolds, Oliver Goldsmith and many other members of the Blue Stocking Club.

Under the patronage of George III, Sir Joshua founded the Royal Academy of Arts. The Academy first met in Pall Mall, later at Somerset House and finally in Burlington House in Piccadilly. Provision was made for an annual exhibition as well as a school of art and the King provided funds to be distributed each year 'for the relief of indigent artists, and their distressed families.'

Living in Covent Garden at this time was Richard Wilson. Today he is known as the 'father of British landscape', but during his lifetime he could not make a living from his painting and in the end he sank into direst poverty. The paintings of the Venetian Canaletto, who came to work in London for a few years during the mid-eighteenth century, met with similar neglect until he returned to Italy.

Gainsborough, Romney and Raeburn were the great British portrait painters of the later part of the eighteenth century. Hoppner and Lawrence worked on till the early years of the nineteenth century, by which time Morland, Turner, Cox and Constable, the great landscape artists, were rising to the height of their powers.

Music and the Theatre

Dr Arne was the most distinguished English musician of Georgian times. He lived all his life round and about Covent Garden and was buried at St Paul's Church in 1778. His memorial plaque bears the opening phrase of his best-known song, *Rule Britannia*, although the sailors who ruled the waves for us were as yet receiving scant rewards for their services.

The eighteenth century had little to offer in pure drama. In 1698 Jeremy Collier had published his *Short View of the Immorality of the English Stage* and most people had agreed with him. They were weary of the Restoration drama and for a while Italian opera had a vogue, being presented at Vanbrugh's little theatre in the Haymarket, whilst theatrical programmes degenerated into spectacular shows of jugglers, conjurers and acrobats, interspersed sometimes with a few short dramatic sketches.

John Rich took over the theatre in Lincoln's Inn and made a fortune from *The Beggar's Opera*, which Gay offered to him in 1726. With the proceeds, Rich bought a site in Bow Street and built the Theatre Royal, Covent Garden, which soon became a serious rival to Drury Lane.

George II brought Handel over from Germany and appointed him Court musician. A new theatre was opened for him in the Haymarket, devoted largely to the performance of his music and operas, but when Handel ran into trouble with the management he joined Rich at Covent Garden. Rich alternated plays with the presentation of operas and ballets. Handel's *Ariodante* and *Alcina* were both presented at Covent Garden during the 1730's and in 1736 *Alexander's Feast, Acis and Galatea* and *Esther*. During Lent, concerts of sacred music were presented, for which Handel composed *Samson, Judas Maccabaeus* and *Solomon*: and in 1741 he wrote *The Messiah*.

At Drury Lane, the acting of Charles Macklin and Kitty Clive revived its fortunes and in 1742 young David Garrick appeared. So brilliant was his acting that within a few years he had become joint manager of the theatre and he remained there till 1776. Garrick employed Dr Arne as his musical director, but in 1760 Arne went to Covent Garden, where some of his lyric operas, including *Thomas and Sally, Artaxerxes* and *Love in a Village* were produced. Oliver Goldsmith's *The Good Natured Man* was presented at Covent Garden in 1786 and five years later *She Stoops to Conquer*.

Peg Woffington first acted at Covent Garden but from time to time she would come and play for Garrick at the Lane. He introduced the first Drury Lane pantomimes, in competition with the spectacular pantomimes staged at Covent Garden, in which John Rich had himself created the part of Harlequin.

Acting was still very formalised and Garrick, for all his artistry, still played Shakespeare in eighteenth century breeches and coat, though towards the end of his career he tried to bring a little more realism into stage costume.

In 1776 Sheridan's play *The Rivals* was presented at Covent Garden but the following year he joined Garrick at Drury Lane. *The Rivals* and *The School for Scandal* were both outstanding successes and when Garrick retired Sheridan took over

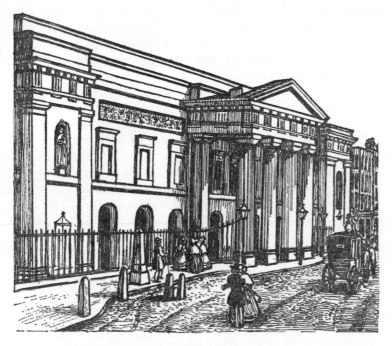

The second Covent Garden theatre in Bow Street. opened in 1809. Later it was known as The Royal Italian Opera House.

the patent of the Lane, continuing the Christmas pantomime. One of his most distinguished actresses was Sarah Siddons and she and her brother, John Kemble, played there for many years, though eventually moving over to Covent Garden.

Sophie v. La Roche visited Covent Garden in 1786 to see the King and Queen, and although a box was reserved for her party the crowds were so dense that 'there was no way of moving forward once on the large stairway; people swayed to and fro as though balanced on the waves, until those above had gained a footing . . . some cried 'I am dying'! 'I am suffocating'. Others lost their hats and cloaks; clothes were torn, arms crushed, and finally the cry went out that pickpockets were among the crowd . . . things were at such a pitch that we were well-nigh flung down the stairs.'

However, they eventually reached their box and of the play itself Sophie merely remarked: 'It was an extraordinary play called *The Belle's Stratagem* and was well acted.'

There were many theatres opened throughout the country in the later years of the eighteenth century, including the Theatre Royal at Brighton and the Theatre Royal at Margate.

Sophie gives an interesting account of her visit to Sadler's Wells in the same year, 1786. The playhouse was, she said, 'dedicated to the small middle-class'. 'This district,' she wrote, 'is very lovely: large meadows alive with herds of excellent cows; lakes with trees in front of the house itself, numerous avenues with delightful tables and benches for visitors, under trees hung with tiny lamps. In the open temple lower-class lasses, sailors and other young people were dancing. We were astonished at the handsome buildings and illumination of the

Sadler's Wells Theatre, 1780

hall, consisting of some hundred splendid Argand lamps, which were bright as sunlight, and proved at the same time that such lamps do not smoke one little bit.

'The scenes in the pit and boxes we found as strange as the ten-fold comedy itself. In the pit there is a shelf running along the back of the seats on which the occupants order bottles of wine, glasses, ham, cold chops and pasties to be placed, which they consume with their wives and children, partaking while they watch the play. The front seats of the boxes are just the same. In three hours we witnessed nine kinds of stage craft. First, a comedy, then a ballet, followed by a rope-walker, after this a pantomime, next some balancing tricks, an operette, and the most miraculous feats by a strong man; another comedy, and finally a second operette.'

Wren's Drury Lane theatre had to be rebuilt in 1791, as it was no longer safe structurally, but in 1809 this third theatre was burnt to the ground in a disastrous fire. Benjamin Wyatt's fourth theatre was opened in 1812 and a year or two later the brilliant Edmund Kean came to act there. London's intelligentsia flocked to hear his Shylock and other great Shakespearean roles, yet the prevailing taste was still for musicals, spectaculars and melodrama.

Covent Garden theatre was destroyed by fire in 1808 and Handel's organ and many of his and Dr Arne's manuscripts were lost. Robert Smirke's new theatre was built to replace it and John Kemble opened with programmes of Shakespeare alternated with opera. Henry Bishop was his musical director and he adapted many of Scott's novels as operas. Kemble also revived several of Arne's and Handel's works, as well as *The Beggar's Opera*, and audiences of late Georgian times heard for the first time Mozart's *Don Giovanni* and *The Marriage of Figaro* and Rossini's *The Barber of Seville*.

John and Charles Kemble both adopted more realism in the presentation of historical plays, and in 1823 Charles made theatrical history with a production of *King John* in medieval dress and armour, which was as nearly as possible authentic.

Pleasure Gardens

Vauxhall Gardens had been the height of fashion in Stuart times. They were still popular in Georgian days and continued till well into the nineteenth century, but Ranelagh was the place to go in the mid-eighteenth century. The gardens, which had once been part of the Earl of Ranelagh's Chelsea estate, were bought privately and turned into a place of entertainment. The famous Rotunda was opened in 1742 and here the fashionable could eat, drink, promenade, listen to concerts, dance and watch the fireworks and illuminations in the gardens. Walpole wrote that 'everybody that loves eating, drinking, staring or crowding, is admitted for twelve pence' and two years later he declared that: 'Every night constantly I go to Ranelagh, which has totally beat Vauxhall. Nobody goes anywhere else – everybody goes there.' However, its glory was short-lived. The 'top ten thousand' ceased to find it amusing and in 1805 the Rotunda was demolished and the gardens dismantled.

Ranelagh Gardens, showing the Rotunda, which was opened in 1742

INDEX